MOSAICA PRESS

It's Okay to Laugh Seriously!

A SPIRITUAL PERSPECTIVE

GITTY STOLIK

Mosaica Press, Inc.

© 2016 by Mosaica Press

Typeset and design by Rayzel Broyde

Revised edition, 2016

ISBN-10: 1-937887-99-5

ISBN-13: 978-1-937887-99-5

Published and distributed by:

Mosaica Press, Inc.

www.mosaicapress.com

info@mosaicapress.com

Printed in Israel

Dedicated to all those who are trapped behind barriers physical or emotional, especially when they have been forcibly and unjustly imposed. Ki b'simchah seitzai'un… we will emerge from these barriers through joy and with joy.

In memory of my parents,

Tzvi Hersh ben Ben-Tzion z"l

Rivkah bas Tzvi Hersh z"l

They showed me passionate, vibrant and authentic living.

Dedicated to my family, from my eldest son down to my youngest grandchild who keep the laughs flowing at all times, headed by the family chief, my husband, who shows us all how to live with serious lightness. May G-d grant them all continuous good health and success, materially and spiritually, and unending reasons to rejoice and laugh.

May all Yidden be blessed with revealed good both physically and spiritually and the ultimate good — Geula Shlaima Now!
L'iluey nishmas our beloved grandmother,

Yetta bas David Bach a"h

May our beloved parents and family be blessed with perfect health and long, meaningful, joyous years!

Avraham HaLevy ben Yetta Levin שיחי'

Yehudit bas Sara Rivka שתחי'

Sara Elisheva bas Yehudit שתחי'

Daniel Yitzchak ben Yehudit שיחי'

Zahava bas Chana שתחי'

Yakov Calev ben Zahava שיחי'

Elisha David ben Zahava שיחי'

Zoe Chaya bas Zahava שתחי'

Rivka Leah bas Alma Bander שתחי'

Mindy bas Rivka Leah שתחי'

David ben Mindy שיחי'

Perez David ben Rivka Leah שיחי'

Yitchak ben Rivka Leah שיחי'

Milton ben Claire שיחי'

Dedicated by:
SHOSHANA bas YEHUDIT and
EPHRAIM ben RIVKA LEAH BANDER

Dedicated in memory of

R. Avraham Leib
ben R. Yakov ע״ה Gralnik

Niftar on leil Shabbos Kodesh, 5 Sivan, erev Shavuos 5775

ת.נ.צ.ב.ה.

In honor of

Yehudis bas Helen תחי׳ Gralnik

May she go from strength to strength and be blessed with long,
healthy, happy years — until and with Moshiach — that are filled
with only simchas, Chassidishe and Yiddishe nachas from all of the
children, grandchildren, and great grandchildren, and abundant,
open, and revealed physical and spiritual good for the entire family.

Lovingly dedicated by
Avraham and Devorah Hayman

Table of Contents

Acknowledgments

Thanks to…

My husband who patiently humored my love affair with the computer, and consistently models how to be serious about your commitments but not take life seriously.

Thanks to the wonderful editing team at Mosaica Press and the vision of Rabbi Yaacov Haber. Special thanks to Rabbi Doron Kornbluth for his great cheerleading and keen eye, his unfailing courtesy, and persistent encouragement. His belief in this project and assurances that "you can do it" enabled me to do it!

Thanks to Mrs. Sarah Balkany for her uncanny ability to discern what's missing, and point out small changes that make a huge difference. Thanks to my daughter-in-law Pessi Stolik, the go-to person for every dilemma, whether editing or otherwise, who "just knows" and is patiently available.

Thanks to Yocheved Lerner, Ilana Mantell, Chanie Banishewitz, and Mushkie Sandhaus for making time for "consultations" to help find just the right word, to rearrange the phrasing, or to clarify a passage. Thanks to my *mechutan* Rabbi Zalmen Marosov for his "humorous" humor input, and to my family for providing me with my daily dose of laughter, much of which found its way into the pages of the book.

Thanks to Rochel Kaplan for her talent with book titles. We all agree that It's Okay to Laugh!

I wish, above all, to express my thanks to the One Above; for from where did any of the thoughts flow, if not from Him? Moreover, He helped me articulate those thoughts. My unending gratitude to the clear instances of His Divine Providence through the entire process.

Introduction

One day, the phone rang.

So what? My phone rings constantly, incessantly. This time was different.

No, I didn't win the lottery... but in a way, I did. That phone call changed forever the way I perceived humor, its value to the community, and to my personal life as a committed Jew. I was privy to an inner glimpse of its power to etch holy, indelible writing onto the human psyche.

Every well has its source, its spring that feeds its supply. The decision to write this book on joy, down to its title, sprang into existence minutes after I picked up that phone one September day.

"Hi, Gitty." It was my cousin Shani.

We rarely speak, but when we do it's always a treat. "I must tell you, your *mechutan* is a genius!"

"Hmm." *Which mechutan*, I wondered? I esteem them all. Mystified, I awaited further clarification.

"Your *mechutan* pretends to be a simple person but he's an absolute genius. We need more teachers like him."

What exactly got her so excited? Shani's daughter, a freshman in a new high school, had come home and offered her mother an enthused blow-by-blow transcript of their *Navi* (Prophets) teacher's comments that had made the class laugh — no, roll with laughter — on his first day. The same thing happened during his second class.

Ninth-grade students often need forceps to extract information from them, but this student was so enthused — it just came pouring out!

That's when I realized that humor is very serious business.

Humor, of course, is an auxiliary of *simchah*. The need for more *simchah* has been gestating in my mind for several years now. Some of the greatest Jewish leaders of our times have made joy their focal points. The Baba Sali[1] said, on more than one occasion, that Moshiach's footsteps could be heard at our doorstep and we should prepare for the Geulah.[2] He often focused on the importance of being happy. Shortly before his passing, his attendant reported, they were eating the after-Shabbos meal called *melaveh malkah* together. The Baba Sali was in a state of enormous joy and elevated spirits, though he had been in pain and unable to eat all Shabbos day. The attendant asked, "What is it that makes you joyous?" The Baba Sali told him that very soon Moshiach would be coming to redeem us.[3]

Increasing our joy levels, we are told, will usher in the Geulah itself. The Lubavitcher Rebbe said:[4]

> The thing that was not yet done to bring Moshiach is the proper avodah (service) of simchah, joy... Obviously, simchah in and of itself is connected with serving G-d, matters of Torah and mitzvos which make the heart rejoice, but the simchah itself should be emphasized — not (only) those things that lead to simchah but the simchah itself, and the simchah will bring Moshiach...
>
> Since this is so, the way to bring Moshiach is, seemingly and not only seemingly, [but] that is the actual conclusion of the matter, through increasing pure joy, simchah, that will bring Moshiach.

The world needs to hear about joy. With all the difficulties of life, we'd all be depressed without a focus on happiness. For this reason, joy has always played a major role in our collective survival. We can become more joyous — and we must.

Still, I wondered: *Is it possible?* Can we tell a person to not only maintain, but actually *increase* in *simchah* in a hurting and hurtful world? We're barely able to keep our heads above the waters; can we realistically be expected to become more joyous? My cousin's account exposed a new angle, a far-reaching, powerful effect of humor that was not to be taken lightly (don't miss the pun). Her excitement and detailed rendition evoked in me a breathtaking epiphany as I realized that, "Wow! Humor is that compelling!" The message was too important and potent to keep to myself.

I had discovered ingredients that would make the "joy objective" more doable: Invite humor and its co-conspirator laughter into the arena! Laughter and humor are the twin engines that keep joy humming — sustainable joy!

In short, humor became the springboard for this book and for life with more joy than ever. It's funny, because I'm not naturally that funny. I can probably generate a good joke at the rate of one (or two) every year (or two!). You'll be able to calculate how long I worked on this book just by counting my jokes, sort of like the age rings on a tree.

Why write?

So how did I get enmeshed in a project like this?

Someone said that people who write do so for three reasons: They need the money (who doesn't?); they're looking for something to do to fill the long winter nights; and they have a message that they think the world needs to hear (hmm).

My writing income so far could barely cover a month's rent, so scratch number one, and G-d knows my winter nights were pretty full already, so I had to stretch them even longer, often into the wee mornings. But that's the price we pay, and with G-d's help; the time was well invested. Because there's reason #3; the message is an urgent one. If it was the message that prodded me, that message cannot be overstated. It is as short and succinct as: We need joy to get out of *galus* (exile)!

Humor reminds me of how my mother would *shep nachas*⁵ as Israel's productive potential developed. A system of irrigation pipes crisscrossing the rocky terrain transformed its arid, unproductive desert into green-bedecked slopes and a flourishing agricultural economy.

That's what humor does. Through the cunning wells of humor, a dry and parched moment bursts into a vibrant, life-enhancing event.

In essence, humor fertilized this book into existence. As I am not a naturally gifted humorist, I too must learn to laugh and smile, to remember to stoke the pastures of joy, to remain perennially blooming and perpetually budding, whether within a classroom's walls or for all-around life. With humor, an average nondescript lecture becomes captivating and uplifting. With humor, the unpleasant issues looming over our lives become more palatable.

Thus, my joy-journey began.

After months of careful shaping, selecting, patting and molding, I sent the material to the publisher. It was a book about joy, with a forty-five-page appendage touting the wonders of humor and laughter.

"Great stuff," the editor wrote back several weeks later, "but even better, could you take those humor and laughter articles at the end and expand them into a full-length book? The laughter and humor material is new and novel and I think the world needs to hear this first. The joy book can be published after this one."

Groan. Just when I thought I was finished!

And then I thought: Maybe I should take my own advice. Maybe I should try some humor to get me moving and to spark the brain. If it doesn't work for me, what business do I have preaching to others?

I discovered what the world already knows: joy demands effort!

I also discovered... that humor works! Gradually, an idea came to mind, and then another. G-d was helping me solve the puzzle, piece by piece.

Did you notice? "I" began the last few sentences. But then "I" discovered that when I bring humor and joy into my life, I make the shift and realize that life is not about what I need and what works for me. It's about a greater good.

The new book and the new "me" have taken shape together. I humbly offer it (us) to you.

Prologue
It's Okay to Laugh

Humans have a primal, insatiable need for joy. Keeping upbeat is an ongoing venture. This is why funny people are popular people. The speakers with the most humor are the most sought after and the most successful. They make us laugh, and they help us move forward. Laughter and humor are important survival tools.

Laughter, humor, and joy are all bound together. Humor leads to laughter, which leads to joy, even though you don't need to be happy to be funny, and you don't need to be funny to be happy. It is a perpetual cycle, as the joy produces more laughter. Sustainable joy!

Consider...

Seven days without laughter makes one weak.[6]

Men need laughter sometimes more than food.[7]

Not to worry, a man isn't poor if he can still laugh.[8]

"With the fearful strain that is on me night and day, if I did not laugh I should die."[9]

Don't you agree?

We all agree that we need joy and laughter. We need them for the little problems and the not-so-little problems that could puncture our mood and spirit. Jews probably know more about *tzores* than any other people. (I won't burden you with mine right now, and I can't possibly hear all your *tzores* all at once, but isn't it lucky we can all laugh at the same time?)

And yet laughter is not a simple matter. Some people want to laugh but can't. Some people can laugh but won't. Case in point: At the end of a laughter event, participants crowded around the laughter facilitator to express their thanks for a refreshing evening. One woman worried, "But I thought we're not supposed to laugh during the *galus*." Was she just a joy-killer or is there a basis to her plaint?

Suddenly I was faced with a question: Is it okay to laugh? The answer: It's not okay to laugh… at a funeral. Otherwise, the question itself is cause for laughter. Laughter is not a luxury; it is so often a necessity of life. It seems more on the mark to ask "Is it okay *not* to laugh?"

Question: Is it okay to laugh? Answer: It's not just okay — it is **necessary**.

The challenger's point was not unfounded, though. We are cautioned about laughing too freely, in deference to the destroyed Holy Temple.[10] What if someone was born with an irresistible funny bone? Does that make him the bad guy or the party champ? What *is* the official policy of traditional Judaism?

Laughter is not a new, hi-tech research discovery. It does not need a panel of rabbis to convert it to Judaism. Jewish laughter was recorded as far back as Abraham and Sarah. Laughter is a dominant theme surrounding the unfolding drama of their life's dream, the birth of their first child.

To formulate a policy about laughter, it's important to get the whole picture. It can be misleading to look at sources superficially. Here's an example of how tricky this can be:

King Solomon, in Koheles (Ecclesiastes) makes several statements that seem to contradict each other: In one verse he says, "I have praised joy,"[11] while elsewhere he questions, "What does [joy] accomplish?"[12]

In one place, he declares laughter as praiseworthy.[13] Later, he claims that "anger is better than laughter,"[14] implying that laughter has little value.

In truth, there are no contradictions. These verses are simply different sides of the same coin. For example, there is a joy that is itself a mitzvah, revelry performed to gladden the heart of the bride and groom at a wedding.

King Solomon's statements scorn joy that is not associated with a mitzvah, while his praise of joy and laughter approves responses that are spiritually related.

"Anger is better" means it is preferable to experience the anger G-d expresses to his righteous followers in this world than the laughter He visits on evil people in this world. "Laughter is praiseworthy," refers to Divine laughter; G-d laughs along with the *tzadikim* in the world.[15]

About that line in the Talmud warning us not succumb to a mouthful of laughter, relax! Don't add this to your list of things to worry about, and don't cancel your teeth-whitening appointment!

When is it okay to laugh?

Here are some ways we could make G-d smile when we rejoice.

Rebbe Nachman of Breslov writes that a person should use joy for pointless activities, such as dancing and other (permissible) sources to generate *simchah*.[16]

The Lubavitcher Rebbe said we should strive to bring ourselves to a state of *simchah*, even from material sources, and then apply the joy to our performance of mitzvos, but warns that this does not include *holelus* (wild and empty mirth), because even if the person feels happy at the moment, he will regret it afterward and be left with the opposite of his intended mood.[17]

Reb Naftali of Ropshitz would walk up and down the beis medrash, scrutinizing his followers. Once after the conclusion of the prayer service he articulated two responses. One was approving, the other disapproving: "I saw Reb Tzvi the *shamash* (beadle) dancing with great ecstasy. He can dance, and it is not in vain... But quite in contrast to him, I saw another man... dancing. What a pity to wear out a good pair of shoes on dancing of that sort!"[18]

The Rambam wrote: When rejoicing on Yom Tov, don't allow yourself to overdo your drinking and frivolity with the claim that you are increasing *simchah*, for this is not *simchah*, just wildness and foolishness... Serving G-d cannot be wild or drunk.[19]

There are several opinions in the Talmud about how much laughter we could roll out of our mouths and into our lives. Here are two mainstream opinions:[20]

The Rambam espouses joy all year long.[21] One should not be constantly laughing, but happy. When a person is overly high and laughs excessively, it is often a sign of inner discontent and suffering. We should refrain from loose behavior when in mixed company, as "jesting and lightheadedness accustom one to lewdness."[22]

The Rama considers joy so essential that he concludes his addendum to the *Shulchan Aruch* with the injunction "*tov lev mishteh tamid*" — one should maintain a celebratory demeanor at all times.[23] There are two opposite expressions of laughter. One from the side of holiness, which stems from the joy of one's connections to G-d, and another that is substance-less, vacuous frivolity (*kalus rosh*). It leads to licentiousness,[24] and should always be avoided. To prevent the holy brand of joy from degenerating into purposeless and unrestrained frivolity, or in simpler words, wild and foolish behavior, we ground our joy with fear of G-d.

Seems it's okay to laugh and be happy at all times — desirable, even. What a relief!

So what is it that often constricts our grins and ties a noose around our smiles?

"There's not enough to go around," some people think, as if G-d created the world with limited supplies. It seems that way sometimes with money, or the housing shortage, or eligible men, so maybe with happiness too. How much happiness does G-d have in the bank, after all? We protect ourselves so it won't be too painful when the limited supply runs out.

"Who am I to deserve it?" others say. It's about poor self-worth. I'm not good enough and my actions don't measure up. This is full-blooded Jewish guilt. Indulging in happiness produces more guilt that I am happy though I am undeserving.

When we feel that we don't deserve His goodness, we tiptoe cautiously around joy, and our smiles are correspondingly inhibited.

Therefore, we only partially open our mouths when we smile or laugh. "After laughing comes the crying (*noch lachen kumpt veinin*)," our mothers would warn us when we got too wild — and mothers are always right. Someone did invariably end up getting hurt and the tears tamed down the rowdy behavior real quick.

Perhaps someone we know is in a terrible situation. How could we be happy when our neighbor is enduring misery?

Maybe we've suffered in life and based on our past record, we find it hard to believe G-d has goodness in store for us. Yes, of course there is so much to be grateful for, but we've gotten accustomed to negative thinking. It's almost comforting. "Most people would rather be certain they're miserable than risk being happy."[25] We're afraid that when G-d sees that we're happy He'll send us new *tzores*. We almost hope He won't notice when things are going okay. (Perversely, "We fear the things we want the most!"[26])

Now is a good time to laugh.

While it's true that our present condition is not as it should be (and that we are living in the **"Every day above ground is a good day." Let's celebrate.[27]** shadow of a destroyed and not yet rebuilt Holy Temple), there is so much we *do* have. The gift of life, I guarantee, is something each person reading this has.

Anything we have in addition to life is a gift from G-d as well. We have G-d's love and personal attention, confirmed by the many instances of Divine Providence in our lives, and the list goes on.

So we would laugh more if we would only *feel* like laughing. It all depends on the mood of the moment. It depends where in life we're coming from and where we're headed. Are we headed from a party to a funeral or from a funeral to a party?

Where *are* we headed? Towards joy or misery? Are things getting better or are they getting worse? Many things seem to be getting worse. Anti-Semitism is **What a wonderful life I've had! I only wish I'd realized it sooner.[28]** on the rise, terrorism, global warming, identity theft...

Our world view is based on where we *think* we're headed. As Peter Diamonds,[29] a futuristic engineer entrepreneur said, "There is no problem that can't be solved. We are headed toward an extraordinary world."

That works for us; as a nation, we are a pretty forward-thinking crew. All we've been thinking about since we've been around is about the future in store for us. We're obsessed with a happy ending to our present miseries.

Did you know: The anticipation of what we expect to happen tomorrow is so powerful that it can override the mood prevailing today? Studies have shown that anticipation of a happy event affects the brain's pleasure centers as much as the event itself.[31] Merely thinking about something exciting to come in one's life can increase endorphin levels, also known as our "feel-good" hormones, by twenty-seven percent!

"My interest is in the future because I am going to spend the rest of my life there."[30]

> Thinking the future will be good, makes us happy now, as wise Winnie noticed:
> *"Well," said Pooh, "what I like best," and then he had to stop and think. Because although eating honey was a very good thing to do, there was a moment just before you began to eat it which was better than when you were, but he didn't know what it was called.[32]*

Ahh, wonderful. What's better, the changes go beyond the minutiae of our own everyday lives. Harnessing our powers of anticipation can have a global impact on our current lives. If a tsunami is a negative result of a relatively mild surge miles and miles away, think of the positive changes that we could precipitate.

Now more than ever...

We are at the precipice of change. We can elicit more than the foamy waves that surge across intercontinental waters. We can initiate good-vibe waves with a forward-thinking mode that will make sweeping changes in the quality of our family lives, among our friends and neighbors — in short, our communities — that will sweep pollutants from a grit-filled world and allow a pure, unadulterated light to shine through. (Did you notice how quickly forward-thinking upped our worldview?)

Something to look forward to, don't you think? I feel my endorphin levels rising. How about yours?

The voice of the optimist: "I intend to live forever. So far, so good." [33]

In the chapters that follow, we will explore the parameters of our joy, laughter, and humor as we anticipate forever-after laughter.

Section I:

Laugh to Live

-1-

Get Me Out of Here

S uppose someone offered you an invention that is sharp as a knife, yet flexible, pliable, and reversible. It rivals Houdini in its ability to release someone from the deepest prison and can save people from dire catastrophes. Would you be interested?

The good news is that you already have access to this amazing product. It is called humor.

When events in your life make you cry, "**Get me out of here**!" humor responds to the plea. Humor is the great Houdini. It liberates us from a cycle of negativity into a place of joy. It is vital for any of us trapped behind a physical or emotional barrier, whether forcibly imposed or self-generated.

> *In a town in Poland there was a Jew who made his living as a burglar. Late one night, he inadvertently broke into the house of the local rabbi and walked in on the holy man hunched over his holy books. When he heard the noise, the rabbi looked up and was surprised to see the burglar. He asked the man, "What are you doing here?" The quick-thinking thief responded without hesitation, "I have a question for the Rav." "In that case," asked the rabbi, "what is your question?" The burglar asked, "What is the quickest way out of here?"*[34]

Granted, this burglar got himself into a mess. He had a valuable tool, though, and it wasn't his lock picker. He used humor to salvage a sticky and volatile situation. In life, we get into plenty of messes. How does one get out of a mess? With humor!

Many jokes are actually clever, witty remarks that pop into our heads in a desperate moment to extricate us from a tight spot. The salvation comes out of the blue like a flash of lightning. In other words — directly from Heaven (we have to give credit where credit is due).

Reb Hershel of Ostropol,[35] a legendary humorist, was always at his wits' end scheming how to earn bread for the day as he kept losing jobs due to his pranks.

His wife woke him up once at night, "Hershel, I hear someone moving around. There's a thief in the house!" Reb Hershel groaned, "*Oy vey*, a thief? I'm so ashamed. He's going to discover that there is nothing to take."

Reb Hershel eventually found the perfect position: a *badchan* (jester) in the court of Reb Baruch of Medzhibozh. Reb Baruch of Medzhibozh suffered from depression, a result of his intense desire and thwarted efforts to bring the Redemption. Reb Hershel's creative wit restored Reb Baruch's well-being. Reb Baruch proclaimed that Reb Hershel had "redeemed him."

> This is not a book about thieves but about humor. Let's resolve not to allow anyone or anything to rob us of our humor.

We thank G-d daily in our morning blessings for our sense of humor. It is the blessing of *matir asurim*, that "He releases us from bondage!" Humor provides a paradigm for mental flexibility to see things from a new and fresh perspective, solve problems in creative ways, adapt to changes, and handle mistakes constructively. Isn't that redemptive?

Ki b'simchah seitzai'un...[36] We will emerge from these barriers through joy.

Humor is not a goal. It is a medium. It is like a spice rather than the main dish. A plateful of oregano delicately laced with salt, paprika, and curry is unpalatable (and laughable), while a dish with no spice at all is woefully blah. We're looking for a happy medium: "serious" food subtly spiced and lightened with a redemptive zest. Humor is a medium, but an amazingly powerful one. Humor is needed at work, at home, on the road, in hospitals, and treatment centers.

Humor is essential for raising children — especially when you want to be heard.

Humor is critical to maintaining *shalom bayis* (a peaceful home), to help mates deflect the foibles of daily and occasional irritations. "It is possible to forgive someone a great deal if he makes you laugh."[37]

If humor is a medium, what is our goal? Humor gets us "out of here." It plays an important role in getting us to where we need to go. Humor could help us navigate the windy roads of life with its sharp curves, steep ascents, dark tunnels, hair-raising roller-coaster rides, and Ferris wheel fortune-turns. (And, in typical illogical-humor form, we could do all this from the comfort of our couch at home!)

Erev Shabbos Mode

Change is chaotic. Visit my hectic kitchen on the day we transition between the workday and the wonderful world of Shabbos. The soup is simmering, the cake batter baking, the chicken burning, the cabbage shredding and... and the clock is ticking. None of these things happen by themselves, of course (with the exception of that ticking clock, which won't stop). Such a mess! I still have all these pots to wash, dry and put away, counters to clear and wipe down, the floor to wash. *Oy*, I almost forgot to cook the gefilte fish. What's Shabbos without gefilte fish? I rush to the refrigerator to find it.

My teenage daughter walks in. After helping herself to a piece or two of the by-now-depleted kugel, she eyes the dining room table with its generous number of place settings, and asks, "Do you have enough food?" She is preying on my weakest point. The kugels and side dishes always look so diminutive when we're in our hungry *erev Shabbos* mode. True, experience has proven that we'll have plenty of leftovers. It happens every week.

Nevertheless, she has pushed my buttons. I'm getting ready to snap some defensive answer. *Oy*, I forgot something else!

My humor! Why is it that just when I need my humor most I forget I have it? Where is it in this dizzying mess? Don't I have a stash of *erev Shabbos* jokes handy by now? I know, I'll check the computer. I keep humor in my computer. I rush over to the computer desk in the corner of my dinette. One joke is all I need. Too late. The computer has been closed down for Shabbos. *Aha, six days a week we Google and on the seventh day we (eat) kugel...*

And, in the delightful anticipation of those wonderful Shabbos foods, we already "kugel" on Friday afternoon. It's actually a mitzvah to sample the foods.[38] Experience has taught that it's wise to make an extra kugel just for Friday, often bigger than the one being served on Shabbos. "Don't worry, Miri, dear," I soothe her, with serene strength, nourished by that Google-kugel concoction. I couldn't have read it on a blank screen... how did I come up with it? I know where it came from. G-d, thank You for sending that flash of humor just in time. "There will be plenty of food for Shabbos. We always have enough. And now, let me check on the soup. Last week it was under-salted."

I carefully lift the lid on soup that is simmering — and shimmering with joy. Humor has made the shift and the peace of Shabbos wafts through my home.

The Shabbos kugel is an analogy for the joy of Geulah (it's just as easy as turning Google into kugel), and the chaos of a Friday afternoon is the perfect time for a foretaste.

Shabbos comes in two sizes: the twenty-four-hour size and the one-thousand-year size.[39] And right before it comes, we crave and need it most.

Each day of the week represents and corresponds to one thousand years of history. In the *Zohar*,[40] the following prediction is recorded:

> In the... sixth millennium, there will be an opening of the... gates of wisdom, preparing the world for the seventh millennium [i.e., the final Redemption], like a person who begins to prepare himself for Shabbos on Friday, when the sun heads downwards. This is because with the coming of Moshiach, "the earth will be filled with the knowledge of G-d."[41]

> *A man walked to the top of a hill to talk to G-d. The man asked: "G-d, what's a million years to You?" G-d said: "A minute." Then the man asked: "Well, what's a million dollars to You?" And G-d said: "A penny." Then the man asked: "G-d... can I have a penny?" And G-d said: "Sure... in a minute."*

The transition doesn't have to be a turbulent event. It can be a serene shift of perspective.

It's All in the "How"

"How we do it" can outweigh what we do. Judaism is about a relationship (with G-d). That relationship should be marked with love and joy.

> I was handed a wonderful four-page publication called *Welcoming the Shabbos Queen*.[42] It informs its readers that "it is a mitzvah to greet the Shabbos as early as possible."[43] "The earlier we bring in Shabbos, the more blessing we draw upon ourselves," blessings such as success in finding one's soul mate and conceiving a child, and more... What is true all six days of the week applies even more powerfully on *erev Shabbos* (the hours prior to the onset of Shabbos).
> - *A childless couple was finally granted a child, but the baby was born with a defect. The Chofetz Chaim*[44] *gave them a spiritual remedy: by midday on Friday, the table should be set. The Shabbos candles should be lit at the earliest possible time allowed by the law. Their son was fully healed, against all odds.*
> - *Parents of a child who had become estranged from his family began to light candles earlier and then sit down to recite Tehillim, as they were advised by the Gerrer Rebbe. Within weeks the son returned to his home and his heritage.*
> And finally, it reminds us, greeting Shabbos in a state of joy is a most exalted way of honoring it as well. We could appreciate the impact of a happy house smelling of Shabbos even before it arrives. The message is softly stated but clear. Shabbos is so important that we embrace it with loving anticipation even before it comes.

Everything that applies to Friday afternoon can be applied to the "*erev Shabbos*" of Geulah.

G-d derives great delight (Divine *nachas*[45]) from *how* we treat the Shabbos. The teacher in me has already prepared the question for the quiz: *How* do we prepare for Shabbos? Answer: Early, with a bonus for adding "with joy!"

And that's exactly how we prepare for the Geula.

Joy is our *erev Shabbos* pre-Geulah kugel.

And that's the purpose of this book: to help us rejoice more, and rejoice now, to laugh more — now. If joy is our kugel, let's get cooking!

It's time to don Shabbos clothing now...

We now have an extra reason to rejoice. Information that was communicated over 200 years ago has just now become known, telling us that we are on the verge of the joyful transition from the *galus* world to the Shabbos of eternity. Apparently everything has its right time, and that time is right now.

Rav Yitzchok Chover, a disciple of Rav Chaim of Volozhin, said that the Vilna Gaon zt"l revealed, shortly before he passed away: When the Russians will conquer Crimea, it will be a sign that the "bells of Moshiach" are ringing — a heavenly bell reminding us that we are now in the time just before the coming of Moshiach. And when they will reach Constantinople (as Istanbul was known in his time), it will be time to put on our Shabbos clothes and not take them off again, because Moshiach will be coming at any minute.[46]

-2-

Excuse Me, Are You Joy-ish?

Do you pass the Joy Test?

I was in my house, and going about my daily housework. My dear mother, who was visiting from Israel, was keeping me company in the kitchen. We chatted as I wiped down the counters, straightened up, swept, loaded the washing machine and transferred the clothing into the dryer. Suddenly she asked me, in Yiddish, "Du zingst nisht — You don't sing while you work? When I got married," she continued, "I would hum and sing when I did my housework."

I put down the toddler overalls I was folding on the table and stared at my mother incredulously. I was silent, but my thoughts were tumbling like the clothes in the dryer that was clacking in the background... My mother who lived through the Holocaust... sole survivor of her immediate family... married in a DP camp... sang as she worked, a few short years after her family was decimated...

Do I sing? Not really. And if I don't, does that make me unhappy?

Yes, my mother was a happy person, with a spunkiness that life couldn't dampen. She forged on. She cried, but she laughed as well, and as time went on, she chose to cry less and laugh more. And she built. And she did not allow bitterness to taint and define her life.

I could not compare my sheltered upbringing to her tumultuous life. And yet, was I happy? And that is the question I am passing along to you:

Are you happy? (Hmm, excuse me for getting personal and putting you on the spot.) I have been asking myself this question over the years, and I'm still in the same spot. Let's figure it out together...

Incongruous

If you saw a person wearing a raincoat, rain boots, holding an open umbrella, walk past your house on a bright sunny day, what would you conclude? This person is clearly out of touch with reality.

Rain does have a quirky incongruousness when we're in touch as well.
- *Little Berry walks into his classroom wearing a single glove. His teacher asks him what he's doing. "Well ma'am," says Berry, "I heard the weather forecast. It said it was going to be sunny, but on the other hand it would get quite cold."*
- *For every drop of rain that falls, a flower grows. And a roof leaks and a picnic gets rained out, and a car rusts and...*

- *What goes up when the rain comes down? An umbrella.*
- *Into every life some rain must fall. Usually when your car windows are down.*

In a sense, *galus* and joy are as incongruous, but in reverse. It may be raining problems on our heads, and nevertheless we're urged to be joyous, wear bright smiles, and walk with light carefree steps. Are we not out of touch with reality? Are we perhaps missing the wisdom and sensitivity of those "realists" who sigh all day over their *tzores*?

We almost feel naïve if we're always happy. Many "smart," grounded people who claim to be more "in tune" with the difficulties around us might sniff down at us: "How could you be happy? Don't you see what's going on around you?"

Unfortunately, I do, especially since I'm writing this on a "bad day." There has been a rash of tragedies in the community. As I wrote this book, two young women that I knew passed away and left families of young orphans. The grief is still fresh. Another lost a husband who was the life of every party (every loss is searing but, in some ways, it is that type of person we can least afford to lose). Let's be honest — joy is no simple matter when you have an older daughter to marry off, or are in middle of an unpleasant crisis, or lonely, or lost your job.

There are probably more reasons to be *un*happy than happy.

Commandments of the Heart

And yet, we're told to "serve G-d with joy."[48] Which leads to the obvious question: Can joy be imposed and summoned up at will, like flicking on a light switch?

A similar question is asked regarding the mitzvah to love G-d. How can we be commanded to love? One can command an action, or a thought, but not an emotion like love and joy! Wouldn't it be nice if, when remodeling my house, I could have the electrician install two extra light switches on my dining room wall, one for love and one for joy?

We are not commanded to "turn on" love — or joy for that matter (should we just call it joyous love?). Rather, we are commanded to dwell on thoughts that will arouse us to love.[49] When we reflect deeply and vividly how the great G-d has selected us from all the nations and how privileged we are to merit and enjoy a relationship with Him, these thoughts will yield love. And that joyous love will be the stimulant to turn on our system.

The Tunnel

The people who suffer deeply will smile and laugh again, but will they be happy inside? Sometimes, as we travel through our various tunnels in life, life looks brighter than it did before we entered when we reemerge at the other end. We appreciate our blessings more than ever.

Sometimes the tunnel is extra-long and windy. And though they have physically reemerged into a sun-drenched world, they are still engulfed in its dark cylinder — residual tunnel trauma lingers (as in the case of PTSD[50]). Physically, the people are continuing on down the road of life while the sun is shining, but their minds are still trapped in that tunnel they traversed earlier in life.

And yet, from the depths and shadows of the tunnel, joy could emerge. We forge ahead. We cry and we build.[51] We are unstoppable. We have optimism and unflagging confidence in the ultimate goodness of our future. We "water new growth with the rain of our tears" and use the "*davka*[52] streak" with which we obstinate Jews are amply endowed to surge forward. Every loss becomes a catalyst for exponential growth.[53]

We turn failure into success again and again — aided and abetted with humor:

How to be a success at failure:

"I wish I had 100 customers like you."

"Are you making fun of me? I know I am a slow payer."

"No, I'm not making fun of you. I really would be better off with 100 customers like you. The trouble is that I have 200."

Manager: From your references I see you've had four jobs in the last month. Applicant: Yes, sir, but doesn't that show how much in demand I am.

A salesman was dismissed because he was rude to a customer. A month later the sales manager spotted him walking about in a police uniform. "I see you've joined the force, Steve," said the sales manager. "Yes, sir. This is the job I've been looking for all my life. Here the customer is always wrong."

Teacher: Everything you do is wrong. How can you expect to get a job when you leave school? Pupil: Well, sir, I'm going to be a weatherman!

Will these orphans and widows, and survivors of various traumas, never smile again and laugh at jokes, even at life? They will. They will *davka* smile and laugh and seek out joy opportunities, as my mother did. Don't even try to stand in a Jew's way (or in the way of the sharp-edged wit that has helped Jews laugh at themselves and trek on).

"I have known sorrow, therefore I may laugh with you, my friend, more merrily than those who never sorrowed upon earth and know not laughter's worth..."[54]

We have been swaying to the tune of suffering throughout our history. It's nothing new.

We have not had, since day one of Creation, a time of perfect joy. Even the two glorious Holy Temples were not complete in their joy. If they were perfect, would they have been destroyed?

It's time for change, don't you think? It's time we get to feel what perfect joy feels like. When, oh when, will we finally celebrate the full glory of our restored Holy Temple? While that can only happen when the world changes for good, we can liven things up now. The kugel was already made, remember? There is extra joy available to tap into at this very moment. Remember, we're actually *advised* to taste the Shabbos foods on *erev Shabbos*. And when we liven things up around us, it sparks up G-d's initiative to shake more joy down on us. That's what G-d does. He matches our moods.

A Creative Art

Our lives lend themselves to two tiers of happiness — or joy, as we prefer to call the luxuriant Divinely-sourced treasure.

The natural state of the soul is a radiant sliver of G-dly bliss. But eventually, our youthful innocence becomes "jaded." Some of us may even become cynical. Gone is the joy of the "why-*not*-be-happy, everything's good" innocence. What takes its place?

In its place will come a deeper joy, a joy that knew suffering, and through it, knows G-d in a brand new way. It's a joy of wisdom, built on the building blocks of pain and experience.

We don't allow tragedy to define us. We harness it to refine and strengthen us. "Strength and joy are in His place"[55] — how splendidly Ezra the Scribe captured the power that propels all. With an indomitable determination we get from the G-dly generator of strength and joy, we pull out new energies from the recesses of our system and we reenter the world of joy. We bring down new light. We *create* more light.

> **G-d gives us very strong hugs. We may say, "Ouch!" but they're hugs nonetheless.**

To truly rejoice, we need the contrast.
"In order to have great happiness you have to have great pain and unhappiness. Otherwise how would you know when you're happy?"[56] Joy that is created from the darkness... what a striking contrast. "The light that follows the deepest darkness burns the brightest."[57] There is so much joy in our lives right now (and we are filled with gratitude for each of those blessings.) And life will get better yet! Because, though things are good, life is not yet perfect. The joy we know is not perfect yet, either. A baby is born, but a beloved family member is laid to rest. A job was found, but a close family member got sick. But we are approaching an era of *perfect joy*. Things will go from mixed-good to perfectly-great.

The joy we pull out, despite all these so-called nasty things that happen to us, proves — to ourselves, no less than to G-d — that our belief in Him is real and enduring. We offer G-d the joy we pulled out of the darkness, and we offer to Him our heart — whole despite the "hole."

We face Him, metaphorically, showing that we are ready to receive. And we do receive... joy, the Divine "amniotic fluid."

Furthermore, we activate (more of) His *simchah* when we practice *simchah*, like a reflection in the mirror.[58] You smile at the face in the mirror, and it smiles back to you.

It's a two-way street.[59]

When G-d considers how faithful we remain despite our assorted *pekalach* (Yiddish for "packages," though here it means burdens), His love for us is reawakened and rekindled. And He gives to us more than we give to Him.

Do two-way streets really measure the same distance each direction? Enjoy this wisdom from a traveler:

> *A recent arrival to the United States was planning a trip to Philadelphia. "Tell me," he asked a friend, "how far is it from New York to Philadelphia?"*
>
> *"About 100 miles," answered the friend.*
>
> *"And from Philadelphia to New York?"*
>
> *"Why, it's the same distance, naturally."*
>
> *"What's so natural?" retorted the immigrant. "Backwards and forwards is not necessarily the same distance. For example, from Purim to Pesach is one month. But from Pesach to Purim, isn't it 11 months?"*

Joy, then, is a creative process and endeavor. Yes, joy is an art. And it is, arguably, the greatest form of creativity available to man, with opportunities freely available every day.

Back to our question... are we happy?

Are we joy artists?

In order to become joy artists, we will need answers to some fundamental questions:

Do I *have* to be happy? Life deals out its "cards." Sometimes I like the cards I get, sometimes I don't. When things are going the way I like, my joy will flow. Otherwise... I'll just "deal," but don't count on my good mood.

Furthermore, could my joy just be my own inner business, my personal secret?

Finally, how do I determine if I'm as "happy" as I could or should be? And whether that joy is authentic?

The chapters that follow will shed light on our questions. But more exciting, we will learn how it is within our reach.

-3-

Oh, to Be Happy Enough

Does joy have a "minimum" required amount, like the amount of wine needed for Kiddush? Jewish joy is certainly not less important than Kiddush. As a matter of fact, the *simchah* of a Jew is so important, says the Rambam,[60] that "whoever refrains from this rejoicing is worthy of retribution." He supports his position with a verse from the Torah:

"Because you did not serve G-d, your L-rd, with happiness and a glad heart... when [you had an] abundance of everything. So you will serve your enemies... in hunger, thirst, destitution, and while lacking everything..." [61]

That sounds severe, doesn't it? At worst, serving G-d in a joyless way should *diminish the reward*. Why does it invite punishment?

I'll venture to say that the Jews were not completely unhappy. After all, it is hard to imagine that an entire nation was completely unhappy!

The Ari, *z"l*, Rabbi Yitzchak Luria, explains that even though the punishment comes for the sins, had the Jewish People served G-d with true joy and happiness, that happiness would have caused Him to overlook those transgressions, regardless of how serious they were.[62]

It is safe to say that for the most part, we as well are somewhere on a continuum of joy. We are all happy at one time or another. The question is, "Are we happy *enough*?"

That question presents a technical difficulty: How does one measure happiness levels? An abstract concept doesn't lend itself to being measured like cake ingredients in a measuring cup.

But if the *simchah* levels of the Jews were not "enough" to stop our eviction from the Land of Israel, "How much is enough?" becomes a critically important question.

How will we know when we've done enough?

I had asked a relative with a sense of humor to share some humorous anecdotes. He sent a few. Then, an hour later, another few. An hour later, he wrote: "I just sent you another one... But, PLEASE, tell me when to stop..."

> *Oh... speaking of when to stop... Someone asked the shamesh (beadle) in shul: "Why does a shul need an east wall (the east wall is reserved for the respected members)?*
> *Shamesh: If there were no wall on the east... all the people who think they belong in the VIP section wouldn't know where to stop.*
> *I never did write him "Enough," but for some reason the jokes stopped coming.*

We need concrete guidance to translate "enough" on a concrete, practical level. Since there is no calibrated joy level, no measuring cup of joy, no height mark on the wall chart to indicate how high our dance-jumps should be, we need some way to know that we are doing "enough" to fulfill the Divine requirement and lead rewarding lives.

Each person has his personal standard and "ceiling" of what to consider "enough joy," based on nature-nurture experiences. Some people are naturals at joy. Others seem to tend towards negativity. Most are middle-of-the-way types who fluctuate between high and low moments.

What's your style?

When the Rambam calls for "the joy that we should rejoice," he provides an example of extreme joy: a description of King David's ecstatic dancing.[63] These are no sedate stately steps. They conjure up an image of extreme capering joy — wild dancing, leaping, whirling and twirling! The message we were intended to hear is: let King David's extreme joy be our model for the type of joy we should aspire to.[64]

In other words, each of us should be clearly joyous. Not simply content. Not simply "keeping our heads above water." Clearly and actively joyous.

You'll know you're doing "enough" when it shows. Don't be afraid to make a fool out of yourself (when necessary). Even you dignified, black-tied and bow-tied men, and you dainty ladies on heels, let's get moving. It's time to see some more of King David's dancing. Let yourself go, but the key is to allow the "know-who-you're-doing-it-for" awareness shine through.

The Newest Scoop

So, how do we increase our joy-levels? With the latest scoop...

The latest scoop is the notion that humor and laughter can be hooked up with joy, and together we'll lick the challenges of life.

Speaking of scoops, allow me to share my ice cream experiences:

I walked into an ice cream store and asked the man to give me a kid's portion ice cream cone. He said that would be a problem, as they sold kids' portions to kids only. I explained that I was a kid at heart; it's just that I have an adult weight (a little overweight, to be frank, which is why I was asking for a kid's portion).

This convinced the person to give me the kid's portion, a cone with one scoop. Well, I finished that ice cream too soon. It had hardly made a dent on my pleasure barometer. And now it was barely a memory. I wanted more.

As a child growing up, my family owned a restaurant. I would sit on a bar stool at the counter in the store and watch them make sundaes. They would put three scoops of your choice flavors into the tall, flared glass, and then add the toppings: pineapple chunks, syrupy walnuts, whipped cream, chocolate syrup, and a cherry on top. Eating a sundae like this was an event.

Many things can make you miserable for weeks; few can bring you a whole day of happiness.[65]

You were satiated for days to come.

One scoop of effort at increasing joy may give me as much mileage as a kid's scoop of ice-cream. Three scoops should do it. Laughter, humor, joy. That will keep me satiated for days.

Kosher Supervisor [Mashgiach] on Premises

But wait, not so fast. Don't they say that humor and laughter are *leitzanus* — vacuous occupations? We're just going to sit around and tell jokes? And laughter is so loud. Some people's guffaws are like explosions. It's all so crass.

Some people are afraid of giving in to joy because they're afraid they'll lose control and things will get out of hand. But we are dealing here with real joy — a joy that is experienced and permeated with an awareness of Whom you are rejoicing for. Where we have that joy, the Divine Presence can enter. Where there is that joy, one does not stumble.

This is why laughter needs to be taken seriously! That's right, we have to be seriously joyish and joyishly serious.

We're going to laugh like never before, but we're going to install an internal kashrus supervisor, a *mashgiach temidi* to be on alert at all times. Humor and laughter are going to power our serve-G-d-with-joy endeavors. We'll have a refresher on what to order up that will make all partakers tingle with delight. We'll be rolling, but no one's heads will be rolling, so that no one will be left out of the fun.

We're going to laugh like never before, with the powerful extra two scoops that lurk in laughter and humor.

Everyone thinks of changing the world but no one thinks of changing himself.[66]

Approved by the Department of Health for the Body and Soul.

Let's Get Going

A young boy that stayed in our house shared a Torah thought at our Shabbos table. Its simple message is well-suited for persons of every age, but the best part is its bottom line: *"G-d said to Avraham our*

Father: the child that will be born to you should be named Yitzchak." Rashi *explains that the name Yitzchak is based on "tzechok" (simchah — happiness), which describes how the father felt after hearing the news that he will have a child at the age of 100.*

After Yitzchak was born, Sarah said: "Kol hashomei yitzchak li" — all those who will hear the news that I gave birth will be happy for me.

The lesson for us is that we have to serve G-d with simchah. We have to learn Torah and do mitzvos not as if we are being forced, but rather to do them with pleasure.

Our joy should be so obvious that it should cause others to be joyous as well.

Don't you love that last line? The little boy modeled the lesson well, as was obvious by the delight with which he recited the Torah thought he "had" to share at the Shabbos table (for homework).

So, let's begin with ourselves, and our change will radiate out to the world around us.

- What will change? Our internal world and our external one, our inner and outer joy...
- We will hook up our body with our soul for maximum joy production.
- We'll challenge our "wits" to take us even further.
- We'll take you beyond these as well, if you are brave.

So let's begin.

G-d first created the body, breathed a soul into it, and then the mind began to function. We will fill our systems with more joy in the same sequence that Man was created. We'll build body joy with its appreciation of the practical and tangible, we'll massage joy out of the soul, and we'll maneuver the witty mind around the knotty passages.

Happiness is self-serving. *Joy* is the way we serve G-d. So, we ask not, "Are we happy?" We ask, "Are we joyous?"

Joy is Divine. Happiness is the pursuit of a lifestyle: comfort, security and well-being. In pursuit of "lifestyle," we invest in material things, gadgets of every kind and size.

G-d made Man.

We will make Man joyous.

Happiness is like a bottle of seltzer. The fizz goes out and we need to open a new one to get the pick-me-up kick. Joy is guaranteed fizzle-proof. It will fill us in a real way, because G-d is the owner, generator, and dispenser of authentic joy.

Joy demands investment — not money, but effort. The more effort we invest, the more we will grow. We invest in our personality rather than into our possessions.

When we want to change a character trait, the Rambam recommends we go to the opposite extreme. We go above our comfort level.

If you want authentic happiness, go for joy.

We can go above our comfort level even in "feel-good" mitzvah-related activities. For example, we feel good when we give charity, but in order to grow, we can try to give above our comfort level. We give until it "hurts." That kind of hurting is good; it is akin to growing pains. When we have joy beyond our comfort levels when times are difficult, we grow closer to G-d.[67]

I've been so close to G-d all these years it's a wonder He never caught any of my nasty colds. The question is: did I catch any of His blazing joy?

Section II

Joy of the Body

-4-

Where Are those Joy Muscles?

We're flexing our biceps, ready to increase our joy stamina, but... come to think of it, they never taught us where those joy muscles are in our biology or phys-ed classes. If we want to build up our joy "muscles" we have to know where they are. Let's explore...

The real question is: Does true joy lie in physical activities such as dancing up a storm at a wedding or a fresh chocolate doughnut on Chanukah, or is it an inner-based bliss — a spiritual serenity? Is it derived from corporeal sources or is it soul-based?

Purim is a great example of extreme joy. On Purim, as well as during the entire month of Adar, we make a big deal over external expressions of joy: lots of shtick, fun, merriment — if it's not jovially expressed our joy is remiss. It seems like action is all-important.

Sukkos is another major holiday associated with joy. The Sukkos joy during the times of the Holy Temple (which centered on the celebration of the water drawing) was marked by juggling, stunt shows, and other fanfare. Again, action seems to be a primary expression.

A wedding as well is an extremely joyous event in Jewish life (it is third in this list, though not in significance). People dance their hearts and feet out, often nursing blisters the next day. The *kallah's* friends bring shtick such as leis, funny hats, masks, signs, and banners. The men do cartwheels, juggling acts, and don costumes to entertain the groom. In days gone by, venerable sages would dance with abandon at weddings.[68]

But let's turn the question on its head. The shtick, and the singing, dancing and stunt shows are all external manifestations of joy. Is that true happiness, or just the reflection of it?

In other words: Is it our bodies that carry the major thrust of the joy experience, or our souls?

Physical experiences are usually labeled "superficial." The inner, spiritual dimension of joy will obviously be touted as superior to joy derived from corporeal sources. And in a certain way it is. Spiritual joy is enduring. It is not a "here today, gone tomorrow" type of experience.

Can external, physical sources of pleasure and joy feed the inner spiritual one?

The answer seems clear-cut. Of course, spiritual joy is more elevated. But Kabbalah introduces a paradox: the body is holier and more eternal even than the soul.[69]

Meet your body.

Don't treat him as you would a physical enemy; rather, encourage him to become your spiritual friend.

Our body-status has undergone a major reevaluation in the course of Jewish history. In times past, the body was sometimes seen as an obstacle to serving G-d, an adversary that we needed to break. The Baal Shem Tov emphasized that the body could (and *should*) become our ally. It could be drafted to assist us in serving G-d. Chassidic teachings tell us that there is an inherent superiority of the body over the soul.[70] It is a tool to serve G-d. Since the ultimate purpose of creation is to sanctify the physical world, the body offers the means by which to carry out G-d's will.

And, if you are looking for a good investment opportunity, body value is going up now. Body-stock is headed to ace the blue chips with 100 percent reliability of return.

Although the soul is incomparably more refined than the body, in the Days to Come, the hierarchy system as it is now will reverse, as is explained in Kabbalistic sources.[71] The superiority of the body will be revealed, and the soul will actually be animated by the body.[72] No more tug-of-war between the two forces. The body and soul will coexist in harmony like the wolf and the lamb. (And along the same lines, *davka* [specifically in] this physical world, not the upper spiritual heavens, is the place that the true essence of G-d is to be found.)

When we infuse the material with a more elevated purpose, we are satisfying body and soul — and heaven and earth — at the same time.

Every pleasure available to us in the world can be used for material pleasure or spiritual pleasure.[73] (Material pleasure is the enjoyment experienced by the body; spiritual pleasure signifies the enjoyment of the soul.)

Aside from obviously good or bad deeds or objects, we have many so-called neutral undefined "gray" areas of life in which we have free choice. Neutral activities could be elevated to the realm of holy or dragged down into the realm of the profane, depending on what we use it for, even what we're thinking while we're involved with it. (Does anyone sell "motive monitors?")

The Baal Shem Tov taught that whatever a person does, be it eating, sleeping, business, or even leisure, can and should all be a part of our Divine service when done with the proper intentions. "*All your actions* should be for the sake of Heaven."[74] Literally. We can "serve" G-d with joy at all times and in all situations.

This fusion of spiritual motives with bodily activities, enriched by Kabbalistic insights, offers the cutting edge of creative joy in the twenty-first century, and we have a name for it: **Joyfusion.**

You can tell when an emotion is experienced, not only on a superficial level, but that it is critical to the person's existence by the way it affects a person. It envelops even his more physical and coarse abilities, down to the heel of his foot, so that he literally dances. Love, fear, and other emotions,

Joyfusion loves when body and soul move in harmony.

when they are so utterly overwhelming, will involuntarily spill over into physical expression.

The physical body must participate in the joy and thereby elevate the physical inclinations.

Some examples of the body-soul relationship:

- We voice our prayers rather than just reading them with our eyes. The most overflowing heart will not fulfill the obligation. The person has to physically move his lips, that's why Jews *shukel* (shake) when they pray.[75] The phrase "all my bones shall declare,"[76] means that the maximum energy possible should be expended in studying Torah, in prayer, and in performing the mitzvos — certainly in the auxiliary joy we exude in their performance!

  This is the perfect analogy of the body-soul interface. How do we know we have succeeded in our Torah studies, a spiritual activity? When it influences our actions.[77]

- When we wash our hands each morning, a ritual protocol, we are reminded that there is sanctity in all our daily activities, spiritual as well as neutral.

- The body and soul team up for the mitzvos, and also for the rewards: The souls in Gan Eden[78] are receiving reward now for the deeds that were done through the body, but the true reward will be after *techiyas hameisim* (resurrection). They teamed up for the mitzvos and they will receive the rewards the same way.

Seamless Integration

Physical and material — there is no divide, they can mold into one. How do we integrate the two? Let's examine holiday joy models. On holidays (Yom Tov), for example, it is a mitzvah to indulge the body. The Code of Jewish Law[79] directs fathers to buy special treats, jewelry, and clothing for his family members. These increase the excitement of the family on a bodily level.

When the Temple stood, the joy of the festivals consisted of eating [the sacrificial] meat. Now that the Temple is not here, the joy lies in drinking wine.[80] Although the festivals were given for our souls to rejoice in holiness ("...and your people Israel will rejoice in

You"), meat and wine are prescribed to harmonize the moods of body and soul."[81]

Even on holy days, the Torah defers to the need for joy to be physically experienced. We celebrate the joy with G-d in a language that allows the body to participate.

How to Laugh More than Ever Before

The Torah's Rx for joy is to use "as needed," and we need it all year round. I humbly offer my cheesecake story to illustrate the use of corporeal joy to celebrate joyous Jew-dom. (They used to say "the proof is in the pudding." I haven't made pudding for decades, so I guess the proof is out of the pudding and into the cheesecake.)

> *I had bought up a stack of cream cheeses in advance of my daughter-in-law's visit from Brazil. She always buys a hefty supply of dairy products, and since they were on sale... Everyone knows I can't resist a sale. But I forgot to give them to her. If you have lemons, you make lemonade. If you have cream cheese, you make cheesecake, even though we were months away from Shavuos. It was, of course, delicious. Just when it was almost gone, I realized, "Oy, I should have linked it to increasing Adar-joy by telling my family that it was made for the purpose of promoting spiritual joy." All wasn't lost, though. Luckily we had an Adar Sheini that year![82]*
>
> *I made another cheesecake and cheerily announced to my family, "It's a special Adar treat." It was sitting on the counter on erev Shabbos when my Shabbos guest came in with lovely yellow roses. I offered her a piece. While she was enjoying it she unburdened about "so much aggravation" she had these last few days with a flood from broken pipes. She thanked me for "the lift" she got from the cheesecake. See, it works!*

This is a wonderful trick: to link the resources and pleasures plentifully available around us to spiritual end goals.[83] G-d gives us material resources, and we return them to him as spiritual gifts.

We lure the body into joining up with our spiritual interests with a language it understands and loves. We elevate joy by attaching our "happy moments" to spiritual pursuits.

Joy on a Two-Way Street

A two-way street is busier than a one-way. We can increase the joy traffic within us by keeping joy moving in two directions: from the inside out (soul to body) and from the outside in (body to soul).

One joy-route is soul-to-body — tapping into the spiritual joy that is always available through spiritual deeds, studying the Torah, and connecting to G-d in our minds and hearts.

Is there really joy inside us? After all, we can't increase something we don't have to begin with.

The natural state of soul, the *neshamah*, is joy. A *neshamah* is a part of G-d and His Infinite joy — doesn't that say it all?

Joy is not the natural state of the *body*, though. The body is self-absorbed; it wants "more." The joy can't last. So tap into the soul.

Joy is born right there in our thoughts.[84] The same five letters that make up the word *machshavah*, "thought," form the word *b'simchah*, just differently arranged. Once it's born, it can grow.

We can increase our joy by increasing the number of joy-thoughts. An added boon is that these thoughts will override the constant stream of negative thoughts. Approximately 80 percent of thoughts and self-talk are said to be negative. Our minds are always on, so a steady stream of positive thoughts is needed to create a positive flow.

And since it is a two-way street, we have traffic moving in the other direction as well. We can import more joy through external activities.

One of the quickest routes to joy is gratitude. Why not start a gratitude list? Include both physical and spiritual items, events, up-grades. This could be a family activity as well. Add to it daily, and re-read what you wrote so far. Revel in it. An example: when I changed my washer-dryer to a more convenient location, it made things so much easier. So what if I did that a decade ago? I'm still enjoying it (I'd all but forgotten, but in looking for things to add to my gratitude list, the memory of the initial pleasure resurfaced). Here's another example: I reinstalled my computer program recently and, oh, what a pleasure it is to do my work on it now (like write about joy)!

I'll keep rereading the list as I add daily, and by the end of the month, the list will be so long that I will sing out enthusiastically, "How can I repay You, G-d, for all the goodness You've done for me?"[85] Notice the phraseology of this verse. It's not a polite thank you, or even a more heartfelt one. It's got an overwhelmed-with-gratitude gushing quality to it.

And once I arrive at that mode, why back down? I may as well stick with it, permanently!

Prayer. A great book on prayer that I picked up at a sidewalk sale gave my morning prayers a new impetus (*The World of Prayer* by Rabbi Elie Munk, Feldheim). Reading the chapter about the morning blessings helped me increase both the physical and spiritual elements of gratitude. The physical aspects of life are elevated through the spiritual realm of prayer.

I had a new appreciation for a trove of gratitude offerings: our digestive systems and physical wellbeing (in the *asher yatzar* prayer), for our souls returned to us (in *Elokai neshamah*), for our intelligence, eyesight, posture, clothing, for the Torah, for the joy of faith, and so much more. (How grateful I am to G-d for making sure the book was waiting there for me. "How can I repay You, G-d, for all the goodness You've done for me?" I must add that point to my gratitude list.)

A recent houseguest left me with a valuable life lesson. This lovely, humble woman lives with her family in a remote region of the world. Her children were married into prominent families around the globe, each in their own wondrous way. She told me that every day she would 1) *daven* (pray) to G-d for success, and then 2) thank Him as well.

G-d, I venture, likes this arrangement. May He continue to give her much to be grateful for!

We could add genuineness to our joy. We can add to the quality of joy by deepening the experience. Hang around young children and try to catch some from them. Children have an important mission — to bring *simchah* into the world of adults.

Or take yourself to a time and place in your mind where, or when, you felt a genuine sense of relief, that made you feel unbounded joy — a true Purim-like relief that makes you want to go out of your box, like I felt after my miraculous spin on Highway 95:

> *My husband and I were driving back from a lovely Chanukah weekend with our children. We left very early on a foggy morning. Half-an-hour into the trip, a truck sideswiped us and sent our vehicle swerving across two lanes. My husband tried to regain control — and we did, thanks to his cool thinking and excellent driving skills. (I could not resist this compliment opportunity, but we both agree ultimately it was thanks to G-d.) We landed on the shoulder facing the reverse direction, completely unscathed, except for some damage to the car. And it was still drivable!*
>
> *It was Chanukah, a holiday when we celebrate miracles. Not only did we spin like a dreidel that Chanukah, we also celebrated the miracle of lighting the menorah that evening in perfect physical shape. I was celebrating life like never before (that mood lasted for a full week at least, before it began to gradually wane into everyday-ism).*

When I think about those moments, I begin to feel great joy and gratitude. Don't we all have moments like this that we can access?

In how many ways are we increasing our joy? In both spiritual and corporeal sources, we are increasing in quantity, we are increasing in quality.

Smile at yourself and others. Be kind and forgiving. Don't judge yourself harshly. Treat yourself like you'd want someone else to treat you. And smile at others. If you smiled seven times yesterday, smile more times today. And, while I spoke about my attempt to "measure" my daily joy, don't measure your smiles. "She didn't smile at me yesterday, why should I smile to her today?" Or: "Her smile as she passes me is just a six–millimeter smile, and that's what she'll get back. I'll save my eight–millimeter smile for the other person who gives me a nice big smile when she passes me."

And while we are smiling, we encounter yet another way we can increase joy — by moving from measurable joy to immeasurable joy.[86] Immeasurable joy is unconditional, it is not measured by what we "get" or what we think is possible.

Happiness is a by-product of an effort to make someone happy.[87]

Smiling at others. It leads to thinking about others. We'll be happier thinking what we're "needed for" by others, rather than what our own needs are. A day that we made someone's life a bit sweeter was a day worth living. And, tell me, how does *that* makes you feel?

Share good news (*besuros tovos*) about yourself, about your community, about what's happening in the world. A *gut vort*, for example, a Torah thought or little anecdote that could bring pleasure to someone, or maybe something you read last Shabbos...

There are certainly many more ways we can increase our joy in quantity and quality. The good news is that you're not just smiling, you're laughing!

That's great timing, because we're headed that way...

We are going to add two ingredients to our mix: laughter and humor, so that we could practice joy "the Rambam's way," the ultimate way. We have already fused the interests of body and soul. Now we will infuse the fire and passion of joy with the fuel of humor and laughter.

-5-

The Great Act of
Laughter

If you're looking for body action to help create joy and keep it alive, there isn't much out there that moves the body more thoroughly than a good laugh. (A sneeze is a pretty moving experience, and even sends things flying off the desk, but a laugh lasts way longer.)

Our body practically heaves, we chortle loudly, and sometimes we even shed tears. Definitely, laughter is a full-body-engaging activity. We are certainly doing justice to the dictum that "all our bones should declare" (our affinity with G-d).[88]

Humor is a wonderful laughter trigger, but we don't need it to laugh. We can laugh without it as we did when we were infants. And listen closely, adults. You should be laughing more often, even when you forget to, or don't feel like it. In fact, those are the most important times to laugh!

So what, physiologically, is laughter? You'll be impressed how aerobic it is.

All muscles in the center of the body are energetically and intensely activated. One half hour of laughter burns 250 calories. A good belly laugh can give health-boosting benefits equal to ten minutes on a rowing machine. Two minutes of laughter is equal to ten minutes on an elliptical trainer.[90] This makes laughter especially suitable for people with limited or no mobility, in particular for the bedridden. "Laughter is inner jogging," as Norman Cousins put it.

"A good, real, unrestrained, hearty laugh is a sort of glorified [automatic] internal massage... It manipulates and revitalizes corners and unexplored crannies of the system that are unresponsive to most other exercise methods."[91]

Even if there is nothing to laugh about, laugh on credit.[89]

Laughter is an intensely physical phenomenon: The jaw opens wide to accommodate the large amount of air to enter the lungs, the tongue lengthens, and the palate pulls in. The diaphragm heaves in short rapid spasms. The head goes into an upward posture to allow more air to enter the lungs. You may develop a short-lived stomach ache from all that air moving in and out.

The maximally open positions of the palate, pharynx, and larynx support the vocal cord vibrations that result in a sound that is loud and bright, what we call laughter.[92]

- **Health benefit: Lung Workout**. Because of its aerobic properties, laughter increases oxygen intake in the body and gives the diaphragm a good workout. Frequent belly laughter empties the lungs of more air than it takes in, resulting in a cleansing effect similar to deep breathing. Ongoing stress often leads to shallow breathing, whereas the deep breathing of laughter benefits the lungs, digestive and nervous systems, heart and circulatory system, internal organs, and more.
- **Health benefit: Pain Management**. Laughter causes the brain to produce hormones called endorphins, natural opiates. These are the body's natural painkillers and help us to relax. (These are the same endorphins that are released after strenuous exercise and are the basis for the exhilaration of a jogger's high.)

Laughter produces a release of chemical signals in the brain (neuropeptides), including beta endorphins (used as an analgesic in the body to numb or dull pain).[93] It has an anesthetic-like effect on the body, suppressing physical pain and discomfort for up to two hours following a hearty chuckle.[94]

Shared social laughter raised people's pain thresholds. It causes an endorphin rush and the release of oxytocin — the same chemical reactions we have to touch.[95]

• **Health benefit**: **Improved Circulation.** Laughter lowers high-blood-pressure, speeds up healing of leg ulcers,[96] and can help reduce the risk of heart disease.[97]

The phrase "radiating joy" is a result of the blood that laughter brings to facial muscles that become red, nourished, and irradiated. But its nourishment extends past the face. Laughter relaxes muscles, expands blood vessels, and boosts circulation all the way to one's fingertips and toes. Laughter is linked to healthy function of blood vessels by causing the inner lining to expand, and increasing blood flow.[98] The eyes will become more prominent and may well up with tears.

• **Health benefit**: Laughter lowers blood sugar in type 2 diabetes sugar.[99]

Is Laughter Holy?

Laughter is healthful, but is it holy? If we irreverently laughed out loud in middle of services in *shul*, we would be the object of disapproving heads turned in our direction. (Imagine a jolly, cackling outburst during Kol Nidrei!)

Isn't it strange that "filling our mouths with laughter"[100] is the popular forecast of our reaction at the end of the *galus* when we will experience the full revelation of G-d's glory?

We can relate to shrinking back in awe as our ancestors did at Mount Sinai.

Laughter and G-dliness seem a strange or irreverent mix.

Is laughter holy?

Our laughter-filled future categorically establishes laughter as a spiritual phenomenon. I daresay that laughter was created specifically for the benefit of the Jewish nation so that we could serve G-d better.

Many things that were originally created for a spiritual purpose can be misused. Gold, for example. It was created for the glory of the Jewish nation, for use in the Holy Temple and for other holy purposes.[101] That didn't stop people from using it to create idols, hurting each other to get more of it, or resorting to illegal means (and force) to acquire it. Today as well, in our money-hungry society, pursuit of wealth "competes" with pursuit of G-dliness.

We have to remain conscious of its original Divine intent and sacred purpose. Laughter is not an innocuous sport. We should take care not to tamper with laughter.

Laughter, a Personal Physician

"Laughter is a wellness program that everyone could afford."[102]

Whether you're suffering from a specific ailment, such as high blood pressure, migraines, breathing problems, heart problems, vascular problems, depression, or just stressed out, practicing laughter can alleviate your symptoms, and in some cases even completely cure you.

The Chasam Sofer, in his youth, would sit in a beis hamidrash, a house of study, and learn incessantly. One day, a woman came to the shul, approached the Aron Kodesh (the Ark where the Torah scrolls are kept), and began to cry out loudly, pouring out her heart about her difficult plight. Her husband had died, and she was left with little children and no means to support them. She beseeched G-d to help her have the means to feed hungry young mouths. From then on, the young Chasam Sofer's learning suffered daily disruption. Every day this destitute woman would return and pour out her suffering before the Aron. Finally, the young Chasam Sofer hit upon a mischievous scheme so he could rid himself of this disturbance. He hid behind the Aron Kodesh, and when the woman began her crying and entreaties, he called out, pretending to be a heavenly voice, "Become a woman who whispers secret prayers for people with illness and this will be a source of income for you." The woman was thrilled that her prayers were received and that she "merited" a clear response. She dared to ask, "What shall my whispered prayer consist of?" And the voice responded: "You will say Asher Yatzar (the prayer thanking G-d for our bodily functions, recited after we emerge from the restroom)."

The scheme worked. The woman no longer came to the shul to supplicate G-d for sustenance, and the young Moshe was able to resume his days of interrupted studies as before.

Many years passed. The Chasam Sofer developed an abscess in his throat. It was a dangerous condition and doctors were at a loss how to heal it. Some advised him about a Jewish woman who literally performed wonders for people with all types of ailments. "She whispers a prayer and the person is miraculously cured," his disciples told him.

They suggested this woman be brought in, but the Chasam Sofer, suspicious of the source of her curative powers, insisted that they should first investigate which prayer the woman used. His followers ran to the woman, but she told them that she would not divulge the nature of her prayer under any circumstances as that would undermine her source of livelihood.

"It was a prayer I received as a gift from G-d," she explained. The messengers begged her and explained that the great Rebbe's life was in danger, and finally, she agreed to reveal the words of her prayer directly to the Rebbe himself. She was brought before him and told him her prayer was Asher Yatzar.

The Chasam Sofer was quite surprised, as he had never heard of any magical powers attributed to this prayer. He asked her how she learned of the power of this prayer. "It was revealed to me from heaven," she explained innocently. The astonishment of the Chasam Sofer grew even greater. Finally, she told him the full story of how she merited to have G-d "personally" reveal this amazing healing tool to her.

The Chasam Sofer reminded himself of his youthful prank and broke out in hearty gales of laughter. He laughed so hard *that suddenly the abscess in his throat ruptured and began to drain. He was healed.*

One way or another, laughter has healing properties. "A joyous heart does good like medicine,"[103] said King Solomon.

Laughter helps us fulfill the dictum "to watch yourself."[104] And — laughter is a medicine with no side effects!

Ah, the dynamic relaxation of laughter. During laughter, our mind shuts down, and we are totally enveloped in the physical experience. Lingering resentments and intrusive worries about the morrow are forcibly expelled as the laughter takes over. People who laugh regularly have stronger immune systems; they report decreased incidence of flu, sore throats, URI (upper respiratory infections), mitigation and even the complete eradication of migraine headaches and much more.

Is it possible that we are uncovering the magic formula for perfect health in the Days to Come? "Our mouths will fill with laughter" and our laughter will annul all illness.

Laughter fosters emotional balance. The conditions in the person's life may be the same but the response to these conditions has undergone change; the person has expanded his/her facility to deal with challenges that life dishes out so that the person is more optimistic. (Good-bye "big-deal" thinking.)

Laughter is liberating. People who can laugh are often viewed as self-confident, friendly, non-constricted, and expansive. Other positive qualities associated with laughter are: optimism, relaxation, calm, smiling, and patience. The world becomes a pleasant place. (More tempting than my morning coffee!)[105]

How can laughter offer healing when the subject matter is so serious? Just begin laughing and your questions will disappear. Experience how laughter...

- Eases emotions and heals emotional pain.
- Makes us more spontaneous and flexible.
- Reframes and shrinks specific threats and stresses.
- Releases fear, which often masquerades as stress.

- Restores the possibility for clear thinking; redirects the trembling of fear (fear and joy are said to be diametric opposites, rather than depression and joy).
- Relieves anxiety and creates a feeling of safety and wellbeing.
- Clears the anger and fear that accompany life-threatening illnesses.
- Gently releases light anger in synchrony with Torah standards, and makes deeply ingrained anger more accessible.
- Helps depressed people find positive aspects in their situation and make it less overwhelming and more manageable.
- Boosts self-esteem, an important component of addiction recovery programs.
- Laughing together strengthens bonds between people even when humor is absent.

To sum it up: Laughter stands above entrapping emotions; allows us to acknowledge them but treat them lightly; feel pain but not be contained by it. Feel the power of laughter-induced lightness!

It's Nice to Know — Some Laughter Trivia[106]

Dr. William Frey is considered the father of gelotology. It is a term for "the science of laughter" that originated in the 1960s. He showed that even if the twenty minutes of laughter is artificially induced, your body will have the same benefits as after one exercises, it will enjoy a lowered risk of respiratory illness, and that it increases production of endorphins that relieve pain.

In the 1950s, people laughed (on average) twenty minutes daily; now we laugh six minutes daily (I wish! It seems even less).

Chinese laugh more than any other culture. They work hard, play hard, and laugh hard.

People living in Brazil and Cuba smile the most. Scandinavians are the lowest on the smiling totem pole.

People are thirty times more likely to laugh in social settings than when they are alone (and without pseudo-social stimuli like viewing a program). Even nitrous oxide, or laughing gas, loses much of its oomph when taken in solitude.[107]

Thirteen muscles are used to smile but forty-seven are required for frowning. You have to smile nearly a quarter of a million times to make one wrinkle.

People smile only thirty-five percent as much as they think they do.

-6-

Three Ways to Laugh

n previous chapters, we've maximized the possibilities for joy by teaming up the body with the soul. The soul possesses three auxiliary powers through which its intellect and emotion finds expression. These are *thought*, *speech*, and *action*. They will offer three additional potent ways to express our soul's yearnings.

So here are three more ways to rejoice, and three ways to share the inner joy with others:

- Smiling
- Laughing
- Dancing

A smile is a laughter-thought. It tells people that laughter is percolating somewhere inside us. Vocalized laughter is a form of speech; singing can be catalogued under vocal joy as well. And a laughter-action is when the joy has spread beyond the confines of the head and heart, all the way down to our feet.

The Smile

Moshe was coming down from the mountain and noticed how dead serious everyone was. The Jews were overwhelmed. G-d's voice, awesome revelations, the sound and light show (the thunder and lightning) were causing their souls to pass out. No wonder they were so dead serious; they were almost dead — serious. They needed some reviving. "Che-e-se," Moshe called out. And from that time on, we eat cheese on Shavuos — and we smile all year round.

Remember baby's first smiles? We go wild with excitement. Baby was an unresponsive mite and suddenly a spark of human social intelligence emerges. We laugh with glee (notice that not every laugh comes from a joke) and summon everyone in proximity, "Quick, come look, she's smiling!"

And then what happens to all that excitement? Where did all our smiles go? I went on a smile-hunt to try and retrieve some.

My first stop: At a fundraising event at a grandchild's school, I kept an alert eye on people's faces. As I moved around, meeting people of the community (but not many smiles), I thought, *How nice it would be if we kept the thrills at those first smiles fresh as when they were first glimpsed.* I even tried to help recover the art of smiling. I offer you two samples of my efforts:

I had a talk with a lovely woman who told me that she badly wanted to do a facelift on her sagging chin, but the doctor thought she was not a good candidate — not young enough and not well enough. I noticed that when she smiled (she had an absolutely beautiful smile), all of her double chin, yes, *all* of it, completely disappeared. And the sunken cheeks that she wanted to

I've never seen a smiling face that was not beautiful.[108] Moreover, "a smile is an inexpensive way to change your looks."[109]

fill in with Botox actually took on the high cheekbone shape she so coveted. I told her, "Just imagine, for the price of some no-charge, zero-cost smiles, you could look so beautiful." What a bargain a smile is.

Next I chatted with a woman who was very intelligent, but oh-so serious. No matter how hard I tried, I could not coax a smile out of her. Certainly, the subject matter was very serious. She was telling me how sad it was that the neighborhood was changing, going down the drain.

I was finally rewarded with one smile towards the very end of our conversation. It appeared gingerly in response to my comment that "helping people makes us feel good." She responded that she was indeed helping someone get home from the party, and that's when the first smile finally peeked through (proof that helping others makes you happy).

We people take ourselves so seriously. We are so preoccupied with how we feel about... and how we're treated... blah, blah...

Meanwhile, the person we're talking to is busy taking herself seriously as well. She is preoccupied with the very same issues: how *she* is treated and how she feels, so she's not noticing you, except for how it impacts her. It sure adds up to lots of serious people!

Rav Dessler saw one of his students walking around with a long face. "You are like a thief!" he admonished the person. "What right do you have to deprive your fellow human beings of the pleasantness of a cheerful face?"[110]

The solution is to take others seriously. Consider not our own needs, but theirs. It's a shift from getting to giving. We'll be able to smile more often once we take ourselves less seriously.

That same area in the brain that responds to laughter is activated by a smile as well. It is now known that the physical lifting of facial muscles into a smile has a real effect on *one's own* happiness-quotient.[111] The muscles will signal to the brain, and you will really feel better.[112] Apparently, a smile is a trigger as well as a response. A smile is a two-way street.

And a smile is just the beginning. For one, it's a laugh in the brewing. And, once they're shared, most smiles are rewarded by another smile. "If you smile at someone, they might smile back."[113] See, you never even give it away.

Today, give a stranger one of your smiles. It might be the only sunshine he sees all day.[114]

A friend shared this smile story:

> *Tzivia had become acquainted with Leah, a young lady new in the community. Leah complained that neighbors were not that friendly. Her wise friend advised her, "Why wait for them to smile to you? Smile to them and see what happens." Shortly*

afterward Leah reported back to her friend, "I love my block. The neighbors are wonderful." Everything had changed.

Be the change you want to see! Don't wait for people to smile to you.

We always knew that smiling was contagious, but now research has deciphered how it spreads from my face to yours, and from your face to mine. In a recent discovery, our complexly designed brains were found to have "mirror neurons." The neuron in the observer "mirrors" the behavior of the doer, as though the observer were itself acting. We are stimulated when we observe someone perform an action *in the same way* as when we are doing it ourselves. A neurological bond is formed between two people merely by way of observation. Because we are living in synchronization with all those around us, we can impress and be impressed.[115] This brings a new life to the famous metaphor "as water reflects a face…"[116]

How ingenious G-d was to think of the smile. Imagine if your family would have to live with you all these years, deprived of the pleasure of your lovely smile!

The Dance

It was Sukkos in Slonim.[117] The holiday spirit radiated on people's faces. But one face glowed with an even more intense light, and the Rebbe Rabbi Avraham of Slonim, noticed it. The face belonged to a young soldier who was stationed in the town with his army battalion.

The Rebbe questioned him as to what he had done to merit that extra-special glow, but the flustered soldier had no explanation to offer.

"There must be something you've done. Perhaps it has something to do with last night?" the Rebbe queried him.

The soldier told his tale. Last night, he had noticed a sukkah (a religious hut in which we eat during the Sukkos holiday) across from his base. He heard the people making blessings and singing and he was filled with a deep longing to fulfill the great mitzvah of making a blessing over food and eating it in the sukkah and be enveloped in that aura of joy and holiness as well.

That night he was ordered to remain at his post and guard the army camp until dawn, when another soldier would relieve him. "So I decided that when all the soldiers were asleep I would sneak over to the sukkah for a few minutes."

And that is what he did. When he got to the sukkah, he took out a piece of bread he had saved and joyfully whispered the blessings over it. He finished his mini-holiday meal and returned to his post. Thankfully, his absence had not been discovered.

The Slonimer Rebbe heard the story, but was not yet satisfied. Yes, it was an act that demanded self-sacrifice, but there was something more that had not been told yet. He urged the soldier to disclose yet more details.

The young man, a bit uncomfortable, continued, "When I got back to the army camp, I was so happy that I was able to perform this mitzvah that I had to do something. So I began to dance. I danced for joy through the remainder of the night, stopping only when I saw my replacement coming toward me."

The Rebbe smiled and turned to his followers. "All of us, at one time or another, have displayed self-sacrifice to perform a mitzvah. But most of us forget to take the time afterward to experience the joy of performing the will of G-d. Because we don't create a vessel for this joy, it can't enter our neshamos (souls). This young man, however, did create such a vessel through his dance, and that's why his soul is glowing so brightly with the simcha of yom tov (the festival).

Emotions are usually contained in the heart and mind, but stronger emotions call forth additional manifestations that could be expressed vocally, or with clapping or other hand movements. In cases of intense joy the feet as well are stimulated. We "dance for joy." Dancing for joy manifests the most intense inner feelings of happiness, and permeates the entire body from head to foot.

Dancing, in the Jewish world, is not a modern-day phenomenon. David whirled away in ecstatic dancing before the Ark. He was thrilled that the Holy Ark, which had been in captivity by the Philistines, and was miraculously returned to Jewish soil, was now being escorted to rest in Jerusalem.

The Hebrew word for festival — *chag* — is related to the word *chug*. Chug means circle dancing. The most joyous festival of all, Sukkos, was called *The Chag*. A Chassidic circle dance is done in a closed circle. It does not exclude or limit the number of participants.

The mind, as the seat of cold reason, is too limiting to be an exclusive vehicle to express all the emotions we feel in our communication with G-d (Who is above and beyond human reason). Joy and ecstasy need a more gratifying expression. Human reason becomes a "brake" rather than an "accelerator" for even high-level Torah scholars.

Ordinary Jews who were not scholars also needed a way to express their sincere joy and love of G-d and the Torah.

There was initial opposition to this mode of serving G-d, and like all things in life, adjustments were occasionally necessary. A student of the Maggid, Rabbi Abraham of Kalisk, took expression of emo-

"When it will be with joy and with a dance then it will happen much more quickly!"[120]

The Lubavitcher Rebbe, 5714

tions to exaggerated extremes. The Maggid rebuked that behavior, and pointed out that dancing should not become an end in itself. The ideal is not to suppress feeling but to use it carefully.[118]

In dancing, the entire body moves. The whole body, head to foot is absorbed in the joy and exhilaration of the dance. Reb Nosson, chief disciple and scribe of Rebbe Nachman of Breslov, wrote the following prayer:

King David danced uninhibitedly before G-d.[121]

Dear G-d, if only my heart would be straight with You all the time, I would be filled with joy. And that joy would spread all the way down to my feet, and uplift them in dance. Please, never let my feet falter, release them from their heavy bonds, and give me the strength to dance, dance, dance...[119]

-7-

Everybody Bonds with Laughter

L aughter is a socially oriented phenomenon. It unifies, it creates rapport. When someone reads a joke they enjoyed, they can't resist sharing it and laughing about it with anyone willing to listen. Or they will carefully store it away in their memory to pull out and relish when the moment presents. Families and friends have their own shared jokes that no one "outside" can understand — the "insiders" chortle though no one else knows what's funny.

Even when we don't get the joke, we often get swept along. Laughter is socially contagious — virally so. Contagious is usually a bad word, associated with spreading disease, but laughter transforms it into a positive quality. Instead of infecting other people with bad bacteria, with laughter we get more value for our laugh as we spread it around.

Laughter is not at all a bad beginning for a friendship, and it is by far the best ending for one. [122]

Robert Provine, neuroscientist and psychology professor,[123] studied people's laughing habits in a laboratory-style arrangement. Though he fed his subjects the best humor, he got barely a grudging chuckle or two. They were missing the main humor ingredient: social nutrition. In a social setting, though, when people were circulating naturally, they laughed spontaneously, and their verbal exchanges were punctuated with many laughter incidents.

Next, he studied an intriguing question: "What do we laugh at?" He noted that conversations didn't need much in the way of humor to produce laughter. We laugh *with* people much more often than we laugh *at* jokes. The laughter is a wordless social language, as they say, "laugh and the world laughs with you."

Apparently, only ten to twenty percent of laughter is generated by jokes. Others are generated by simple remarks (personally documented) like, "It was nice meeting you... Have a nice weekend...Thank you."[124] It could actually be entertaining to take note of the comments that are followed by laughter.[125] Here's one I just picked up, "I forgot what I wanted to say... it'll come back later... hahaha."

What is funny about these lines? Nothing really. If we tune in carefully, we will catch the tail end of an internal dialogue that whizzed through our funny-brain. Or it came from an internal cooling system. Forgetting what you wanted to say can be mildly stressful.

A caveat: As in all things, a balance is necessary. Following King Solomon's lead, there is a time to be serious and a time to laugh. A constant stream of facetiousness can lend an artificial aura to life. And be ever vigilant about *holelus*, a meaningless, pointless, purposeless, and barren stream of nothing. Then it would be better just to be silent. "Beware of those who will laugh at everything or nothing." If you have nothing to say, why not laugh at someone else's humor attempts and make them feel good?

Life with humor could be an ongoing song. In his book of Psalms, King David provides us with the recipe to make it so. In the first verse of the first chapter he advises us how to maintain a happy state: "Happy is the man who... has not sat in the seat of scoffers." Technically, any talk that is not linked to G-d's Divine wisdom and Torah is empty talk. The Baal Shem Tov said that when we are "on the go" and unable to study, we must still mentally connect what we are doing with a higher reality.[126] Though we are not directly involved in prayer or study, we can worship Him through non-sacred activities. It could be through a conversation, even a light one. It could be a joke to lighten things up.

Humor is a gift. When we use it to refresh, de-stress, expand, or lighten so that we can be better people and build a better world, it is our song.

Producers of shows know that people often listen to a sound track (either audio or audio-visual) in the privacy of their homes. The contagion of laughter is so powerful that radio production came up with the concept of sound tracks to add the impetus of being part of a crowd of laughing people. The humor feels funnier when you hear others laugh, and your sense of having enjoyed the program increases dramatically. In the U.S., artificial laughter, also known as "canned" laughter is used. These sound tracks convince people the joke is better than it really is, but don't fall for it. Respect your own taste! On the other hand, we should thank people for their efforts in helping spread laughter...

Trying to better understand laughter's effects, researchers measured brain responses to various sounds via MRI scanners. Every type of sound triggered a response in specific regions of the volunteer's brain, but positive sounds such as laughter were found to produce greater responses than negative ones. That may explain why we respond to laughter with an involuntary smile.

What is the point of all this research and findings? For me, one thing stands out: that "people need people" to maintain a happiness homeostasis.[127] Laughing brings us together, and coming together helps us laugh. Doesn't that upgrade the value of one's neighbors and friends?

The Heart in Humor

Humor can be used to bring people closer together or keep them at arm's length. Healthy humor does not belittle or criticize, but is based on empathy and caring. An invitation to laughter is an invitation to share, as when people use laughter in conversations to connect. If laughter is a glue that is meant to help people stick together, let's stick to that kind. "A laugh, to be joyous, must flow from a joyous heart, for without kindness, there can be no true joy."[128]

This is the heart of the humor message.

If the only benefit we get from the information in this book is a heightened sensitivity towards how we use humor, it was worthwhile.

Some people, men especially, use humor because of their discomfort with expressing deeper emotions. Their jokes are a cover-up; there's a heart buried in there somewhere. It's important to find a balance. Humor is useful as a relief, not an escape hatch.

People may become humorists to cope with stressful situations. Benny was an older single whose friends were mostly married. Humor rose to the occasion; he and his other single cronies would joke their bachelorhood pain away. The humor was like an analgesic. Eventually Benny got married, but his wife discovered, to her chagrin, that he was already previously married — to his joke-mode. It had become habitual. Despite her repeated efforts, he deflected her efforts to have a serious talk. When you want someone to listen to you seriously, unending jocularity is painful. His wife finally told him, "If you won't talk to me straight I won't answer you."

There is a time to weep and a time to laugh. Things don't feel as dire, dismal, or daunting when looked at through the prism of a joke. On the other hand, joking about absolutely everything that occurs is not normal. "Constant flippancy is just as wearing as constant solemnity."[129]

Genuineness is a worthy goal in all communications, even when we send the "sharp arrows of our wit" on the wings of those messages. We can tune in to our tone of voice. Is it dry, detached, deprecating, supercilious, or is it flowing from a place of goodness, kindness, joy and a willingness to share? Are we speaking as compatriots or "at" people?

Is your humor "Abraham's "brand" or "imported from Philistines" (Plishtim)?

Our patriarch Abraham was an extroverted personality who exuded love and warmth for all.

The Philistine people,[130] too, were open, gregarious, and exuded joy and love. The two seem similar, don't they?

The name of the Philistine people will cue us in to the difference. The word "Philistine" denotes openness; the Mishnah refers to a passageway that is *mefulash* (from the same root word), that is, it opens to the public streets on both sides. The Philistine personality style is open with no restraint.

Abraham-style joy and humor is always directed towards a good purpose. It will have boundaries, lines that are not to be crossed. Philistine-style joy and humor is carefree. "Everything goes." It has no principles, no goals, and achieves nothing.

A person who doesn't have borders doesn't respect borders and boundaries of others. The Philistines thought nothing of invading other's territory. They seized control of Abraham's wells.[131] They were a menace during the era of the Prophets and captured the Holy Ark for seven months.

Abraham's genre of humor is marked by humility and how it could help extricate people from tight or uncomfortable situations. It is humor with a heart. The humor comes from a sense of caring and wanting to build. Philistine humor is self-indulgent, flaunts decency, and tears down respect and personal boundaries.

G-d did not allow the Jews to travel through the Philistine territory after their Exodus from Egypt. Their sneering and cynical comments are insidious and harmful and damaging to self-respect.[132]

Self-improvement advice:

We often resort to humor as a useful way to sugarcoat a sermon. The best way to talk about improvement is to address it to yourself — oops, I mean myself. If we point our finger at someone else, it grates. If we use our own self as the target we score twice: the person enjoys the process and the message will be more readily accepted.

Mordechai Schmutter, humor columnist in Hamodia magazine (what a talent!), wrote an article decrying the bad habit of permanently adopting books we "borrowed."[133](I've lost many valuable books like that, with no clue to whom they were lent. And I thought I was the only one — it's happened to you too?) After detailing the saga of a particular book he'd loaned away, in the last sentence of his article he experiences a sudden amnesia-reversal. Out of the dim recesses of his memory, he has a startling recollection. The book he is eulogizing is not his at all. He had borrowed it from a friend.

Humor is "Jest a Knife"

Humor is not an intellectual pursuit or edifying topic in and of itself. But it is a skill; creating a good piece of humor does need a quick and sharp wit. That's one reason we call humor "sharp" — sharp and therefore potentially dangerous. Like a knife, we exercise care when using it.

A knife is a most useful and wonderful tool. We'd have a mighty hard time preparing fish or meat or chopping things into usable size without our trusty knives. We have knives for our salads, challah, and for hundreds of other uses. Remember your mother showed you how to transport a knife to the table? Keep the blade facing down, she cautioned, a knife pointed straight ahead may accidentally inflict a wound.

A joke could do that too. A keen sense of humor could lighten, make peace, redeem from misery, and make people receptive. On the other hand, humor and mocking can hurt more deeply than many fancy tools. And the gales of empty laughter are sometimes "thinly disguised waves of howling pain."

Sarcasm is a kind of black humor. Though it can be mild and funny, it often expresses hostility, anger, bitterness, jealousy, frustration, and dissatisfaction with life. Sarcasm is caustic, no matter how charmingly delivered.

Controlling, manipulative types love the sneak-attack of sarcasm. Confident people are happy to express their feelings directly. They don't need to sideswipe.

Some things we don't joke about:

Avi Shulman, in Making Little Things Count & Big Things Better *(K'hal Publishing, 2001), tells about his visit to Seattle, which sits in the shadow of the spectacular Mt. Rainier, one of the tallest mountains in North America. Mt. Rainier is a dominant force in the state of Washington; its picture is featured on the license plates, houses that are built try to include its view in one of their windows. In shul, a guest to the city commented, "I wonder if I could get a Coca-Cola sign on top of The Mountain. That would be a great advertisement!" Suddenly there was silence in the group. The out-of-towner realized his comment hit a flat note; it was not appreciated. He apologized, saying, "I was only kidding about the sign. It was just a joke."*

"Sir," one of the locals said quietly, "we don't joke about The Mountain!"

Everyone has his Mountain. If you lived in the plains of Nebraska, you might have low tolerance for "corn-y" humor (corn production is a pillar of its economy). If only we would respect the people in our lives as much we respect our "mountains."

Humor, like all sharp cutting tools, has its set of do's and don'ts. Laughing *at* others is insensitive; laughing *with* others is good humor.

Never try and force people to laugh. People have different degrees of willingness and different capacities for dealing with issues and traumas they recently experienced.

Don't just sit there and listen if you realize someone has become the butt of a humor-basher. Speak up.

Do look out for phrases like "just kidding." He's not. He was serious; he's just taking the edge off the message. "Can't take a joke?" is a signal that bullying is taking place.

Humor can degrade a person or upgrade a moment. Avoid swiping at issues that a person may be uncomfortable with, like **Every joke has a glint of truth at its core.** body build, complexion, the person's name, a distinct feature. You may think you are kibitzing (just joking), and it certainly will not make you feel one drop uncomfortable, but no one should ever be the butt of a joke, except your own self, and that, too, should be done in moderation.

Which One Is Your Mountain?

Which of these personal features would you *not* appreciate being the butt of someone's humor stabs?

- a balding head
- a doubling chin or sagging jowl
- shape of your nose
- bunions
- blooming waistline
- two left feet

Personality or other traits can also be sore points. Would you want someone to joke about:

- your loquacity
- the business blunders you made
- always losing things
- always late
- can't get the joke
- the mess you leave behind you
- can't carry a tune
- add yours here...

A good piece of advice is to "laugh at yourself first before anyone else can."[135] It may not be easy, because you do need strength to make yourself vulnerable. But look at the fringe benefits: "The person who knows how to laugh at himself will never cease to be amused."[136] And this should really be convincing: "If you don't learn to laugh at your troubles, you won't have anything to laugh at when you're old."[137]

Before poking fun consider this: "Just some harmless fun" is a matter of perspective, it depends who is the one getting skewered.[134]

Make Humor Transparent

Learn to assess the quality of the joking around, and make its motives and underlying message more transparent. People may use humor to disguise a message or a need,[138] or as a substitute for expressing emotions. What is the humor trying to achieve? Upgrade your emotional intelligence by developing a discriminating ear for authenticity of intent.

Is the humor:

...being used as a weapon — as a tool of aggression, to hurt and humiliate *or* as a shield to deflect tension and strife or defuse a crisis?

...trivializing and derailing a (serious) discussion *or* is it invigorating, adding meaning and enjoyment to the conversation?

...being used as a tactic to steer away from a topic they wish to avoid (this may be a signal to be more sensitive in presenting the issue) *or* is it a way to get attention or seek control?

...disguising emotions the person may not want to reveal — fear, disappointment, embarrassment, jealousy, or anger *or* is it simply disguising a message — we won't dare lodge a serious complaint, so we'll toss off a humorous but pointed remark instead?

... a means of self-protection, (for example, the woman who jokes about her weight may be introducing the topic to guard against someone else bringing it up) *or* to suggest to others that she is comfortable with it (her body language should offer clues: is she making direct eye contact or is she avoiding it)?

...reflecting a compassionate attempt to show empathy and understanding *or* is it a veiled criticism, as for example, when an employee arrives late and her supervisor greets her with an acerbic "glad you could join us"?

Of course, humor may be used innocuously. People who are happy and comfortable with life just naturally use humor. We thank G-d we have plenty of happy, comfortable people in our lives and can enjoy the gift of humor as it was meant.

Section III

Joy of the Mind

-8-

In Quest of the Sense in Humor...

What role does humor play? Is it just a language of nonsense to get us laughing? And so we set out in quest of the sense in humor.

We talk about having a "sense" of humor. Sense, as in "perception," is a way of looking at the world, a lens or looking glass, to borrow from *Alice in Wonderland*. If not for humor to help us develop our joy muscle, we would be unsmiling, laconic, cranky, miserable, cantankerous people. We "hire" positive humor to replace criticism.

Humor is classified as a consciousness, which is a sense, rather than an emotion, but it can produce many positive emotions, such as joy, mirth, hope, confidence, and an overall sense of well-being. Its emotional aspect has great healing potential.

Humor has an added pleasure embedded in it: the keen ingenuity of wit. That explains the tag "sense" of humor. We harness wit and use it to overpower life that threatens to overpower us, and also to tame life, control it, and be humbled by it all at the same time.

Could it be that a "sense" of humor is another vital sense in addition to the five we usually list?

Humor describes the ludicrous; wit exposes it by comparing or contrasting it with something else. Humor is "an outgrowth of nature and accident; wit is the product of art and fancy."[139]

Wit, according to Wikipedia's definition, is a form of intelligent humor, the ability to say or write things that are clever and usually funny. Creating a linguistic wordplay is an art and talent as in these examples:

All was rosy for the newly married couple. After a few days though, the wife noticed that her husband was eating with his fingers. The wife tried, in the nicest and most diplomatic way possible, to correct his behavior.

"I will tell you honestly how I feel," said the new husband to his lovely new wife. "I've always felt that if food wasn't clean enough to pick up with your fingers, it wasn't clean enough to eat!"

———⁓———

Reb Baruch asked Hershele Ostropoler to light candles to illuminate the room. He lit one candle. "That's all? One candle is not enough. I cannot see." Next night, he lit five, then ten, twenty, thirty, and he wasn't stopping. "Do you want to blind us here?" asked Reb Baruch. "I don't understand. Yesterday you were against darkness, today you are against light?"[140]

———⁓———

Two people were sitting in the coffee shop discussing what it must be like in heaven.

"One thing is certain," commented one, "we will have a good rest up there. No buying or selling up in heaven."

"You're right about that!" agreed his friend. "That is not where business has gone."

Thanks to G-d for an endless resource in our wonderful wits. And, an infinite supply of opportunities in which to practice them. And if we're ever worried about running out, here's something reliable to fall back on...

A Jewish patient tells the doctor he wants to be transferred to a different hospital.

The doctor says "What's wrong? Is it the food?"

"No, the food is fine. I can't kvetch (complain)."

"Is it the room?"

"No, the room is fine. I can't kvetch."

"Is it the staff?"

"No, everyone on the staff is fine. I can't kvetch."

"Then why do you want to be transferred?"

"I can't kvetch!"

It's nice to know that when you have nothing else, kvetching could stand in as a luxury. We had so little, for so many years of our *galus*, and very little of that as well. But we always had the luxury of having our humor to kvetch with, and thank G-d for that!

-9-

Laugh to Learn. Seriously.

Do we take humor seriously? There is no college degree offered in the field.[141] While we memorize quotable quotes of the notables, we rarely credit a joke with its creator's name. If we collect all the jokes we've ever heard, the one useful profession we could probably gain from doing so is professional comedian. Humor doesn't claim to fill a person with information. It works the opposite way: to loosen us up so that we can digest other information. It also doubles as pain relief — relief from the stress of studying for that murderous exam, knotty project, or crisis that has us stressed out for days.

Humor is generally viewed as the lighter side of life. Relief from tedium is just a joke away. Joking is usually viewed as wasted class time, study time, or work time. "Okay, enough fooling around. Let's get back to studying. We have three chapters left and we're running out of time."

Goal-oriented teachers often shun humor in their classroom. Remember the giggling that disrupted class and had your classmate (okay, so it was you) courteously transported to the other side of the classroom door (okay, not so courteously)?

Here and there, an enlightened teacher knew how to balance a little breath of funniness with the heaviness of the learning atmosphere. Still, many did not. I remember my fifth-grade English studies teacher. She did not crack one smile the entire year until, finally, in June (!) a riffle of shocked whispers rippled through the class. We saw the first smile break through her stern facial mask. Rumored to be a mere seventeen years old, she may have wanted to impress the principal with her professionalism, or maybe she was worried about losing control. Her efforts were a success — we were absolutely petrified of her.

Even the teachers that smiled did not tolerate laughs well. School is for the serious-minded.

The fountainhead for this book was my epiphany about the far-reaching impact of humor — in the classroom and beyond as well. A cousin had called me to tell me how lucky she and her daughter were to have the benefit of this one-of-a-kind teacher, Rabbi Tiechtel, who, she knew, was our *mechutan* (our children are married to each other).

Rabbi Tiechtel wasn't resorting to humor because he loved to entertain but because he wanted to impact sixteen-year-old girls who often love to laugh more than they love to learn. His concern and goals as an educator extended far beyond the upcoming marking period and mastery of the subject matter. In the few hours he had every week, he instilled memorable and valuable life concepts that would become solid building blocks for all their lives. In the first weeks of school, for example, he lay down a concrete application of *ahavas Yisrael* (love for a fellow Jew), built up their self-value, and promoted *simchah* (that calls for a round of applause!).

Rabbi Tiechtel had found a simple but brilliant technique to implant eternal truths. His particular knack for interjecting hilarious humor right in middle of a serious lesson should be patented.

I attempted to interview Rabbi Tiechtel, the humor-genius, but he played down his abilities. At any rate, any attempt to capture his humoristic forays in other than in its natural setting would diminish it.

His humor is never cheap, and never a deviation from quality teaching time. He may artfully spring a totally unexpected question, an almost off-the-wall comment to a random student that is so unexpected that it induces hilarity. However, he succeeds in driving home his message as powerfully as those large rollers that just smoothed the new asphalt down my street. I still remember my cousin's account of several years ago. His students remember them for a lifetime.

Apparently, Rabbi Tiechtel made the commitment to cultivate his students through joy before he ever entered a classroom. In life, he is not the "joker" but a serene, gentle man with a crinkle around his eyes. His specialty is "translator"; he translates life's encrypted challenges into what they really are — messages of G-d's love. People know they could turn to him for a mood-boosting pep talk, but he reserves humor for his students.

Several months after I began working on my book, I got a call from a friend. She had discovered an article she thought I would enjoy: It featured a teacher who had left a lifelong impact on the writer, along with a poignant, personal tale. As my friend read it to me, it became obvious that it was our own humor-hero Rabbi Tiechtel who was featured! How fortuitous that this article found its way to me!

When Rabbi T. walked into the classroom, all the natural boredom, fidgetiness, and irritability that teenagers are known for flew right out the window. It wasn't only his lessons, rich with knowledge and down-to-earth wisdom. No, much more than that, it was his simchah. Rabbi T. was simply bursting with simchas hachaim (joy de vivre) and it was eminently contagious. So much so that its effects stayed with us long after the bell rang.

I will never forget Rabbi T.'s simchah. His face lit up with joy. He walked around like a man without a care in the world... an unparalleled joy. I remember thinking, hoping, yearning to achieve the same level as Rabbi T. and at the same time wondering whether it was even attainable by me.

And then, out of nowhere, the bombshell struck. A young girl had passed away. The funeral was tomorrow. The father was none other than our beloved teacher, Rabbi T. To say we were shocked was an understatement. Our horror and disbelief was confounded when we discovered that Rabbi T.'s daughter had been sick all year! Every day when he walked into our classroom with his signature smile and jovial warm greeting he had been dealing with a dangerously ill child and we had never once known it.

At the shivah house (the week-long mourning period) the experience was surreal. Even as he sat before us on a low stool, Rabbi T. taught us... about the role of the soul in this world... At the time I never imagined that his soft-spoken words would ever have any bearing in my life. True to form, Rabbi T. was back to his teaching after the shivah was over, with the same smile, the same demeanor... My friends and I were in awe.

Fast-forward a dozen years. Rabbi T.'s smiling face never left my mind, even as the vicissitudes of life sometimes made my weary smile fade. While the school I'd attended had been quite modern... my husband and I were now raising our children in a beautiful Torah path. When our fifth child was born, however, life as we knew it ground to a halt. A serious congenital disease left his heart, lungs, spine and other organs terribly damaged... He would need minute-to-minute care, countless surgeries. Our home took on the qualities of an intensive-care unit, but we were endlessly grateful that he pulled through and was alive.

Shortly after his third birthday he underwent another complex surgery... This time G-d claimed this special soul for on High and we were bereft.

We sat shivah, mourning the loss of our beloved child. The house was crowded with visitors. A distinguished-looking gentleman with a sense of purpose that seemed to permeate his very being made his way over from the men's side to where I sat... I looked up from my low stool and — standing there was Rabbi T.! How had he heard? We weren't quite sure. But his caring eyes and nurturing smile were just the balm we needed.

Rabbi T.'s indomitable simchas hachaim, taught through his unfaltering example, imbues me with strength to this very day, more than twenty years after I left his classroom.[142]

There is a personal twist to this saga: It turns out that I knew that little boy (Paysach) very well. As a matter of fact, I had the unforgettable privilege of participating in a warm farewell to him on his last day of school, though we did not know that at the time.

I had been working with some children in the class Paysach attended. The day before the surgery, because of the impending procedure, he had to leave early. His health aide, holding Paysach's hand in her own, got his coat and backpack quietly, intending to make a quiet, unobtrusive exit so as not to disturb the teacher's lesson. The teacher was absorbed in her lesson and did not notice them leaving. I overrode my reluctance to disturb the teacher in middle of her animated lesson (little children's attention could be difficult to recapture), and quietly pointed out their departure to the teacher so that Paysach would get the send-off he deserved. She appreciatively interrupted her lesson, and the boys sang out a warm "good-bye" to Paysach. We did not realize at the time that we were saying our final farewell to this most precious child who had accomplished his mission in this world in a few short years.

If humor is good for learning, wouldn't it be beneficial for every setting, whether in the walls of a classroom or otherwise? A little humor couldn't be bad if the Talmud reports that Rabba would share a humorous remark that would cause his students to laugh, after which "he would sit in awe" and begin to teach.[143]

We are now going to make some surprising — and useful — discoveries about humor.

Keep Thy Humor Holy

As we can imagine, Rabba, a great Talmudic sage, was not the type to enjoy telling idle jokes for the "fun of it." His humorous remarks, as all his informal, casual comments, contained deep wisdom.

Obviously, the conversation of a sage does not fully represent his true depth and brilliance. The humorous remark is merely external in contrast to the deep internal content of his teachings. It serves as a facilitator to the deeper wisdom, much as a father who lowers his hands to pick up his young child so they can interact face-to-face.[144]

The precise expression in the Talmud is: "before Rabba would 'open' [to] his students..." The unusual wording "open" suggests that an effective teacher should first "open" the faculties of his students so that they will be ready to receive his teachings. Rabba did this by prefacing his lecture with a humorous remark.

At a parent-teacher conference, a frustrated teacher lamented to a parent: "As you see from the marks, your child is not performing up to par, although he definitely has the potential. He's missing the all-important ingredient: *cheishek* (a one-word composite of desire and will). If he would only awaken that desire, he would see how pleasurable learning could be."

When a teacher makes a joke, the humor anecdote moves the student into a positive mode and renders him "learning-receptive."[145] In addition to enjoying the sharp wit, the student is now in a state of delight. That delight sparks his *cheishek*.

Let's get on the humor train and see where it takes us: Humor sparks pleasure, which sparks *cheishek* (desire and will).

Speaking of trains, *What's the difference between a train and a teacher? A train says "choo-choo" and a teacher says, "don't chew"!* (Overheard in Rabbi Tiechtel's class.)

The point is made, but oh, so gently. When the teacher shares some humor, it bridges the gap between giver and receiver. He is meeting the student on a relatable level. The connection is made. Not only has the mind opened but the heart, as well, has been engaged.

> **Just as the pupil of the eye expands in response to light, the pupil's mind and heart expands in responds to "delight."**

Impact of a Rebbe's Joke

A Rebbe of many Chasidim would sit with his congregation on Shabbos and discourse for many hours. Once a man wandered into the synagogue, curious to hear some of the wisdom of this noted Rebbe. Suddenly, the Rebbe, in the course of his talk, told a humorous story, and everyone, even the women listening from the balcony laughed. The visitor was a bit put off by this. A Rebbe tells jokes? It seemed unseemly, frivolous. He walked out of the synagogue, his interest in this Rebbe effectively squelched.

Many years later, at his Shabbos table, one of the guests told her story. She was not originally religious. One of her friends had been urging her to come and check out the lifestyle of the Orthodox community. She finally agreed. She walked into the synagogue on a Shabbos afternoon and was struck by the absolute quiet that reigned while the Rebbe spoke. "This place is too serious for me," she thought. Life needs humor. I will have nothing to do with this." Suddenly, there was a burst of laughter from the men's shul. She was in the women's gallery and they too were laughing at what the Rebbe had just said. "What was funny?" she asked and when they shared the humor she laughed along with everyone. "Hey, these people know how to laugh," she thought. "They're alive." And she immediately upgraded her stereotyped characterization of the staid and serious Orthodox Jew. "Maybe here there is meaning in life, and humor as well." She expressed interest in exploring more and today she is a fully committed Jew raising an Orthodox family.

Her host's interest was piqued. "Do you remember how long ago you visited this congregation?" he asked her. It turned out that they were both there the very same afternoon. What seemed frivolous to him turned her on to become a serious adherent. The humor had picked her up — as the father picks up his child.[146]

Telling a joke is an activity that has the potential to be used the right way or the wrong way. It can be a tool to enhance our practice of Judaism or it could be empty, or worse, base. Base humor does just that — it debases.

**Enjoy thy humor
and keep it holy.**

If a person is telling, or enjoying, a joke "for the sake of Heaven," it becomes a good and holy act.

In truth, it's easy enough to have good motives when sharing humor: to cheer up a downcast person, to open our heart to serve G-d with gladness, to avert a crisis in the house, to open our minds to the study of His Torah... there are many examples.

Un-limit Your Pleasure

Why does humor pack such power?

Humor is undeniably a source of pleasure. Is it just a fleeting lift? What purpose does it have in the scheme of our lives?

Humor and pleasure are closely related. Laughter comes from delight, but not all objects of delight cause laughter. We could be delighted at beautiful scenery, but do we laugh? On the other hand, people could laugh scornfully where there is no delight.

Let's take a closer look at pleasure.

On some level, everything we do is driven by pleasure. What a wonderful feeling pleasure is! It pervades us fully when it makes its presence felt. If only we could **Pleasure may not be funny, but laughing at something funny is certainly a pleasure.** push a pleasure button to activate that wonderful feeling and let it wash over us at will. Where does that pleasure-center lie?

Deeply embedded within each of us, in the innermost core of our soul's psyche, is an internal drive for "pleasure." It is the inner gear that drives the other gears that make us tick. When the body or soul "wants," the wish emerges from that central pleasure core that drives the will, and in turn directs our emotions, motivations, and choices.

Neuroscientists know that the neurotransmitter, dopamine, controls our "pleasure" signals, but the intricate interplay between pleasure and will remains elusive. Our mystics don't have to dissect souls in scientific labs to study the intricate link between pleasure and will. They have their information from unerring sources.

We each have our own pleasure palette and preferences, but there is a general rule to ranking pleasures. From lesser to greater, it goes in this order: Good food (I think I hear a hum of mmm) is probably our most common source of pleasure. Sports are a huge pleasure drive for millions of people. Both of these are physical activities. Enjoyment of delights from physical, corporeal sources for its own sake is an animalistic pleasure — animals find them satisfying as well. This doesn't mean that they are bad (not at all!), only that they are limited. A short while after the meal, the pleasure is gone. The food has no long-term redeeming value.

A higher form of pleasure is music. Music and art are aesthetic pursuits. They are partially physical; they still depend on sensory input for their expression and enjoyment. Note that the less corporeal a pleasure source, the more refined and spiritual is its form. Still higher is pleasure from traits of character and emotions, such as the satisfying feeling of helping someone in need.

In every one of these, our motives are not guided by intellect. We are reacting on the animalistic level, the emotive impulse, and in that case there is no consideration of value or sense of purpose.

Superior to all these is intellectual delight. I hear our music lovers protesting, "What can be more pleasurable than music?" Music transports us to heaven on earth, whereas using intellect requires focus and effort — that's pleasure? But the verdict is in. The brain, our crown jewel, and our intelligent soul raises man above all creatures. Intellect reigns supreme.

"Man should find his supreme delight in matters of the spirit, particularly in intellect."[147]

Using the mind to think, reflect, discover, and master a new idea is the highest form of pleasure experienced by the human race. And when we apply it to the study of Torah... ask anyone who enjoys a juicy Torah thought or Torah class how blissful that is. The pleasure is indescribable.

The limitation of pleasure is that it cannot be vicariously experienced. Would anyone rapture over the fragrance of a rose if he never had a whiff? There's nothing like a firsthand experience.

You and I, burdened as we are, deserve some pleasure, and it's there waiting to be sampled.

It makes perfect sense that Man, who possesses an intelligent soul, will find his pleasure in Torah study. It binds two intellects: A person who studies Torah with his own intellect unites with G-d's intellect.

Ah-h-h...

Here's how pleasure and humor work their way into our everyday lives:

Pleasure in its pristine state is a "soul-capability," a *potential* to experience pleasure, not the actual pleasure experience. It does not manifest in a specific organ but quietly controls our system from the center of our being. In Kabbalistic language, it is known as *taanug pashut* (simple, uncompounded pleasure, the *essence* of the faculty of pleasure).

When "pleasure" activates, it teams up with an object of pleasure. For example, when I derive pleasure from a fragrant cup of coffee, the pleasure in my soul (my "soul-faculty" of pleasure) teams up with the sensory pleasure from the coffee in my cup to form a pleasure "composite."

Humor and laughter: A person laughs. Ha-ha becomes Ah-h-h... The system registers the laugh as "pleasure" and links the laughter directly in to this pleasure core, this root of laughter, the "pure pleasure."

Intellectual pleasure is a complex pleasure, a composite of pleasure and intellect. Laughter is a pure pleasure.

Here's how the humor-laughter "chemical reaction" works: A person shares a humorous anecdote. It might be that only a few people double over with laughter, but laughter is contagious. Even those who are initially unimpressed get swept into the spirit, and soon everyone is laughing along.

Once the enjoyment levels have gone up, the trigger, the funny line, becomes insignificant. The "high mode" developed a life of its own, and everyone's on board.[148] The humorous remark fed right into the *taanug pashut*.

The joke is gone but the good mood remains. And that's good news.

> Researchers found that students who were taught humorously scored 15% higher on exams than students taught without humor.[149] Students remember humorous words more often than non-humorous words. They understand the message better and remember it longer when information is accompanied by humor.
>
> Humor seems to enhance learning on a purely cognitive level as well.[150] The understanding of humor is a cognitive activity that engages the entire brain. Humor appreciation stimulates both the left and right sides of the brain. The "right brain" connects a *memory* to the pleasurable laughter event. The "left" brain ties the *content* to a memorable emotional moment.
>
> Researchers have found that "a wave of electricity sweeps through" the entire cerebral cortex (the whole brain) just before we laugh. This supports the theory that humor can actually help improve cognitive functioning by activating all parts of the brain simultaneously.[151]

We have a humor paradox of sorts here.

The external humor is of a higher root, while the lecture is the ultimate purpose. Each one has its *yichus* (status or lineage).

Humor, our errant "child," the distracter and time-waster, is actually the high hat that leads us to serious intellectual growth! All is not lost for you cavorting, gallivanting jolly souls. From humor — indeed, *with* humor — you will progress to scholar. No joke! Humor will make a scholar out of you yet.

> Funny fact becomes a fun fact: With humor, we'll remember more, not less. With humor, we learn better, not worse.

Humor School Handbook

Would you like to join our humor school? Our handbook has a few rules:

1. Relax. Learning to laugh should be fun!

2. Bring your family members on board: the more, the merrier!

3. If you are a teacher, tell a minimum of one joke per lesson. More are allowed.

4. If you are a student, our program is *not* a license to read joke books during class.

5. Joke books will not be allowed into class until the day you hear your teacher say, "Now everyone, take out your humor textbooks and open up to gag #94."

-10-

Brain Food

The illogical logic of humor has so much to offer. Humor is fun — and useful as well. It offers an impressive array of life-enhancing nutrients, an ability to reverse course when necessary, a glimpse beneath the surface, and openness to an entire range of possibilities.

The Torah and humor share common skills. Jews have a "Talmudic aptitude for intricate, ambivalent opinionating." They "revere verbal cleverness over athletic prowess,"[152] and they have multiple answers to every question.

Meet the convergence of the two — inversions and reversibility:

> One fine day, a hunter hunting in the woods came across targets painted on different trees. He was amazed to see that all the arrows had hit bulls-eyes. What an amazing feat! The hunter was curious to meet this unusually talented marksman. He found the archer and asked him, "What is the secret behind your unerring aim?" "It's simple," replied the archer. "First I shot my arrows, and then I painted the circles around the target."[153]

This is an absurd inversion. The arrow is supposed to seek the target, not the other way around. It upends the typical, logical way of thinking. And yet, absurdity has great value. "Absurdity reveals more about the hidden realm of things than any type of rationalism can," writes Nilton Bonder in *Yiddishe Kop*.

This "inversion" kind of thinking skill is very valuable to members of the Jewish nation. The greatness of the Jewish people is its ability to operate with this kind of inverted perception. This was succinctly and dramatically expressed when they proclaimed their readiness to accept the Torah on terms of *"what G-d has said we will do and [then] hear."* Cause and effect were reversed.

Of course, the normal sequence is first to hear and find out what it's about. Then, if you like it, you do it.

From the moment we said "we will do and we will hear," we created a new paradigm. Curiosity usually leads to pursuit of knowledge. Here it followed knowledge. Switching the sequence of cause and effect, creating the answer first and the question second, is a strategy employed in humor called *reversibility*.[154]

Trust in G-d, *bitachon*, operates on the same principle. First we followed Moshe Rabbeinu out of Mitzraim into an uninhabited, uncivilized desert. Then we wondered where we'll be getting our meals from.

Good reversibility skills are necessary for humor — and to be better Jews:

> *Two people came to see the Satmar Rebbe. One person was a bearded Jew, the other a more modern Jew. The bearded Jew was barely acknowledged, but he noticed that the Rebbe received the modern Jew very warmly — unusual, as the Satmar Rebbe was a zealous man. The bearded Chasid was a bit offended, and he protested to the Rebbe.*
> *"I have a long beard and yet, you gave me a cool reception while this modern Jew got a very warm reception."*
> *"I'll tell you the difference," the Satmar Rebbe told him. "When he comes to Heaven, the Heavenly Court will say to him, 'Jew, Jew, where is your beard?' To you, they'll say, 'Beard Beard, where is the Jew?' "*[155]

As in the target and bulls-eye analogy, the two values of "beard" and "Jew" exchange status priority to shed new light on the essence of Judaism.

Sam and Sylvia lived in a comfortable apartment but Sylvia complained and nudged her husband endlessly to look for a nicer apartment in a nicer neighborhood. She claimed that after all these years of skimping and saving they were entitled to a little upgrade. He resisted. Why bother to move to a more expensive place when things were fine as they are? Finally one day Sam surprised his wife with some news: "Sylvia, at last you'll be getting your wish. Starting next month we'll be living in a more expensive apartment." Sylvia was ecstatic. She envisioned an elegant new house in an elegant neighborhood.

"Park Avenue perhaps?"

"Not quite," he responded. "The landlord just raised our rent!"

Did you notice? When the present gets worse, the past gets better. (If only we could learn to truly savor the precious "present" at present.)

Many of our parents or grandparents lived in countries where the police would constantly check their identity papers. This made life problematic because many Jews had to flee their places of residence to evade draft or other "unlawful" activities. Where there are more problems there is more humor, and so Russian country jokes are in great abundance. Here is a story of an encounter between a Communist cop and a *Yiddishe kop* (Jewish head):

Lieberman, who lived in St. Petersburg, had company. His cousin was visiting. However the cousin lacked a residency permit and was worried about being caught without documents if he would be stopped by the authorities. Lieberman tried to calm him down with the following plan. "Here is what we'll do. If the policeman approaches, I'll run away. He'll chase me, and you'll be able to escape."

The plan worked. An officer pursued Lieberman, and when he finally caught up with him, demanded to see his papers. Seeing that the documents were in perfect order, the officer asked: "Why did you run away when I came toward you?"

"Me? Run away? My doctor told me to run a mile after each meal in order to aid my digestion."

"But didn't you see that I was running after you?" asked the policeman.

"Certainly," replied Lieberman. "I assumed your doctor told you the same thing!"

You can count on humor to turn an adversary into an exercise partner. Instead of allowing a a situation to trap us in its web, we get to grab it and tuck it into the net of humor:

I was late to work again today, and there was my boss, just as I walked in the door. Lucky someone was equipped with a humorous definition of "boss." It helped me reverse the down-hill direction of my mood before it spoiled my day: A boss is "someone who is early when you are late and late when you are early."

Ambiguity and Multiple Meanings...

Do you take things at face value? Would you like to sharpen your discernment skills? Jews are trained to examine the precise wording carefully as they study Torah texts and glean information from its multiple meanings. Is it surprising that the members of the Jewish nation, nurtured for generations on creative thinking, are agile humorists?

The ambiguity of not knowing which "next one" falsely propped up this mother's hopes for a blissful few hours:

After they brought their first baby home from hospital, a young wife suggested to her husband that he try his hand at changing diapers. "I'm busy now," he said. "I'll do the next one."

The next time the baby was wet, she asked if he was now ready to learn how to change diapers. He looked puzzled. "Oh," he replied finally. "I meant the next baby!"

My sympathy is extended for that mother's dashed expectations. She's going to have to read this humor section to recover.

Here's another of marriage's authentic snippets.

The wife can't sleep because the window was left open and the room is freezing. Loath to leave the warmth of her bed, she lay there, shivering under her blanket and called: "Aaron, it's freezing outside. Could you close the window?" The husband, tired and half asleep, tries to shut out his wife's repeated requests to close the window. Finally, she succeeds in rousing her husband. He opens an eye and grumbles: "And if I close the window it'll get warmer outside?"

I wish I was as clever in my alert state as this fellow was in his drowsy state. Now, if the wife can think of a quick comeback she might not have to get out of bed after all!

Whose side are we on, actually? I do hate getting out of bed when it's chilly in the room, so I will avoid taking a stand. Whatever you work out, do it with humor! (Anyways, it was just a joke; don't take this too seriously! In our perfect world, spouses are so eager to please their better halves that they jump up eagerly with a smile and even a joke, any time of day or night to help each other — right?)

Humor based on double entendres is best enjoyed in its original language.

"The stork just brought you a beautiful baby boy," the nurse told the new father.
"The stork never brought this baby," declared the young man, staring at the hospital statement. "The bill is way too long."

Hebrew teacher: "That will be all for now, Susie. I have a headache."
Little Susie: "Oh, I know about that. Moses had a headache, too!"
Hebrew teacher: "Moses had a headache? Where did you hear that?"
Little Susie: "From my grandfather. He said G-d gave Moses two tablets."

People who are versed in Torah often use its verses to create a creative and humorous spin on life. This describes my father's brand of humor. He would pull out expressions from the written or oral Torah, deftly applying them to the situation at hand. How I wish I would have recorded some of them to share today.

> A Rebbe was giving his future daughter-in-law a blessing, hours before her chuppah. After he bestowed his blessing, he, in turn, asked her for a blessing. She was a little overwhelmed by the thought that a great Rebbe was asking her for a blessing, but humor helped her rise to the occasion.
> Quoting a line from the Talmud, she quipped, "Al tehi bircas hediyot kallah b'einecha."[156] (Do not regard an ordinary person's blessing lightheartedly.) She had created a pun with a double play on the word "kallah," which means 'light' when spelled one way, and 'a bride' when spelled another way. Thus, the saying was customized to express that a kallah's blessings are not trivial, even though she was humbled by bestowing her blessing upon a tzaddik.

Hidden Meanings...

Hidden meanings... Humor teaches us to recognize the difference between what is said and what is left unsaid. It trains us to be open to covert messages in our day-to-day lives. Do we mean what we say? Do we tune into what was left unsaid?

> The census taker comes to the Rubenstein house.
> "Does Abe Rubenstein live here?" he asks.
> "No," replies Rubenstein.
> "Well, then, sir, what is your name?"
> "Abe Rubenstein."
> "Wait a minute — didn't you just tell me that Rubenstein doesn't live here?"
> "Aha," says Rubenstein. "You call this living?"

And Literal Ones...

Here's a little test of your reading skills:

> *Question: Sema's mother had three children. The first child was named Shira. The second child was named Shaina. What was the third child's name? Answer: Sema.*

> *Question: How much dirt is there in a hole that measures two feet by three feet by four feet? Answer: There is no dirt in a hole.*

> *Question: Before Mt. Everest was discovered, what was the highest mountain in the world? Answer: Mt. Everest; it just wasn't discovered yet.*

If we hone our skills at reading the literal text carefully, we will be less easily misled. On the other hand, being literal doesn't mean we should get stuck to the form that was presented. If we say it's raining cats and dogs, don't alert the mice as well.

The ideal is to not ignore the literal meaning of things, and yet, simultaneously, to remain open to an entire range of possibilities. The following passage is an illustration of that synthesis:

> *Two men were having a discussion: "We live with the constant hope of Moshiach's imminent arrival. Do we all take what we say literally?"*
> *They decided to test this. One of them, Asher, approached a wealthy businessman in their city. "I need a loan. Would you be able to help me out with $3,000?" The businessman had no qualms about giving him the loan, as he was known to be honest and reliable. "I'll be happy to extend the amount you need."*
> *They sat down to write and sign the IOU note. On bottom, Asher wrote, "Payable when Moshiach comes."*
> *The businessman pointed to that line and said, "What is this? This is not a serious commitment." But now he was faced with a dilemma. If he truly lived with the premise that Moshiach*

is coming any day literally, he should have no problem giving a loan on those terms.

Truth is eternal. There are no contradictions, only many possibilities.

Flexible Wits...

There's more than one solution to any dilemma. The Talmudic texts are chock full of different ways of seeing things. And it carries over into our lives. Two Jews, three opinions.

The agility of humor helps us as well to see multiple opportunities in life. We can replace rigid thinking with the ability to flex and s-t-r-e-t-c-h our thinking muscles. Elasticize your mind and life with humor.

> *The customs officer at the border crossing in Tabriz[157] was giving a Jew in the import business a hard time. Each time he brought a wagonload of goods from Germany to the border, the customs officer took advantage of him, demanding mercilessly inflated taxes. The merchant was powerless, as the customs officers could do as they pleased.*
>
> *The situation came to the attention of Reb Moshe HaLevi Segal, known as the Libauer Rav. He asked the merchant what he planned for his next business enterprise.*
>
> *"I am planning to import a large shipment of shoes from Germany," the merchant told the Rav.*
>
> *"Buy the most expensive shoes you can," he instructed the merchant, "but bring only the right shoes to the border. Leave the left shoes in Germany for a while."*
>
> *The merchant brought only the right shoes to the border. The customs officer, noting the high quality of the shoes, pronounced an exorbitant fee. He assumed the merchant would pay as usual, but this time, the merchant did not. He left the shoes at the border.*
>
> *The standard practice was that anyone who did not pay the tariff had his goods confiscated, and they were subsequently auctioned off at a public auction. When the shoes went up for*

auction there were no competing bids, because nobody had use for half pairs. The merchant was able to buy the entire wagonload for a paltry sum.

A few days later, the merchant returned to Germany for the second half of the shipment — the left shoes. The entire process repeated itself. Once again, the shoes were acquired for a minimal price.

Now, the right and left shoes were united. The merchant earned enough to make up for the monies he had overpaid in the past due to the avaricious officer.[158]

A family lived on a farm in a rural area. Life was not easy but they managed to eke out their basic needs with a few cows, goats, chickens, and their vegetable garden. One day, the husband came home excitedly with some good news. "Did you hear, Moshiach is coming! We will finally be going to Eretz Yisrael. No more worries about stolen animals and attacks from the local goyim. Galus is over!" The wife listened to this, and she became quite rattled. Who wants change? Things were going as well as could be expected. "Why do we have to be the ones to leave?" she protested. "Let the goyim go to Eretz Yisrael and we could live here in peace."

People do indeed fear the Geulah, assuming it will unfold through apocalyptic events. Fear and resistance to change stand in the way of progress. Fear is considered by many to be the diametric antithesis to joy.[159] This should sooth our worried, anxious souls: *geulah* and *golah* (exile) share the same four letters, with the addition of the letter *aleph* in *geulah*. The one difference between the *galus* and Geulah is that the "aleph" (*alufu shel olam*, Master of the Universe) will reveal His light. Our perception of His presence will change from *believing* in Him to *seeing* Him. The world will continue to run as before while the positive changes evolve naturally.[160]

-11-

The Joy of Humor

Fresh in my mind is the comment made by Cilia, a woman I met at a workshop. When she heard what my pet subject was, she said: "Humor is *so* important. It brings joy to the world."

It may be stating the obvious, but sometimes the simplest words evoke the warmest glow.

Think back to your own life. The high and memorable points are the ones spent with people with a sense of humor. I had a set of friends in my school years — twins who were hilarious and still are. I have the best memories. Long forgotten is the pressure, the difficulty of sitting behind a desk for hours, and some boring lessons here and there. All I remember is what a "blast" my school years were.

The teachers who used humor will never be forgotten. Those wonderful oases of pleasure will be cherished memories forever. Once, in a maternity ward after giving birth, I had the most fun and liveliest roommate. Those were a memorable two days.

Notice how the speakers who begin their talks with humor have their listeners eating out of their hands. Besides that humor opens people's minds to absorb the information, a speaker who opens his talk with a juicy anecdote has given us a gift, a priceless

> **"There is no common denominator between people I admire, but one with people I love — all of them make me laugh." [161]**

commodity called pleasure. He made us feel good, and now we harbor warm feelings towards him.

With so many advantages, humor can change and enhance every part of our lives, as this story proves:

> *Shoshi had a very frustrating year as a kindergarten teacher. Her classroom was ill equipped, the building was in poor condition, her students were difficult, and the parents were critical. Luckily for Shoshi, her teacher's aide had a great sense of humor and an optimistic outlook. "Every time things got hard, we joked about it. We learned how to laugh at almost every situation." She learned something very important that year, predominantly from her aide: how to see the funny side of life.*
>
> *"Despite all the difficulties, it was the best year I've ever had as a teacher."*[162]

Humor leaves an imprint on the brain so powerful it can outshine life's difficult times. Yes, "a good laugh is sunshine in a house." We forget the difficulties and joy-blockers and those times will actually be remembered in a positive light.

And I thank G-d for sending those funny people into my life. They have lent a glow to my years gone by, and, judging by my mother's oft-repeated phrase that "old age is no fun," we probably need more and more of it as we age.

Some people are naturals, but others have to remember to turn on their humor mode (that's me, I recognize!). We have to consciously move our default setting to humor every so often. That's why we like to hang around funny people; they turn on our funny brain. Suddenly we're seeing another picture — there's a humorous angle we didn't notice before.

So, what is humor adding to the picture? Humor has so many important purposes. Let us count the ways...

Humor Wears Many Hats

Humor is... *a colorist and home decorator.*

Humor adds color to our lives. Some days we feel like we live in a gray world, drab, humdrum, gloomy and glum, a "what's-life-for-anyway?" feeling. This may be a result of extended malaise, loneliness, fatigue, just plain low spirits, or indigenous (part of your inner system) moodiness. Add color to your life. Either share some funny lines or create your own.

Some people live a black-and-white existence. Everything is either right or wrong. There's no in-between: If the plan didn't succeed, it failed. Everything has to be the way they plan it, conceive of it, imagine it. They are going to be uptight more often than you care to know of.

"This is the only way it can be done!" "Do it now!" "The rule is..." "It's wrong, and that's that."

They allow very little wiggle room.

With very little investment, actually, at no cost, we could become designers. Home decorators. Throw in some color. Some like bold and bright colors. Or if you prefer a monochromatic theme... try those pink spectacles. (Imagine if glasses were available in two styles: regular, or with a humor lens, like bifocals! Either type will lighten things up, but the humor perspective will also expand your view.)

> Lady to man in optician store: "I'm returning these glasses I bought for my husband. He's still not seeing things my way."

People add colorful spots to our lives, and humor provides a wonderful burst of color. How about teaming the two — people who practice humor. That combination makes for a real power boost in one's life.

Humor is... *classy.* At any rate, it should be.

Joking about other people is cheap. You have better taste than that. Humor should be directed at life, not at people. At experiences, not at those we are supposed to love and cherish.

Monitor yourself: What was your motive? To make others happier, to clear the air? Or was there a spitefulness at its core? How do you feel after the joke? Cheap and empty or refreshed and light?

I know, there is an endless barrage of husband-wife jokes, and mother-in-laws are favorite fodder, but be classy, please.

(Notice, on the other hand, jokes about one's kids are relatively scarce. How would all the mothers of marriage-worthy children cope if there was no "top" boys for their "best" daughter... which brings to mind the mother who came to her son's school and asked, "Could you please deliver this lunch bag to my little boy?" "How will I know which boy is your son?" "You'll recognize him easily. He's the top student.")

Humor is an art. An important element of art is the concept of "taste." While there is an aesthetic value to humor, taste refers to the distinction between good and bad reasons for laughter. "Amusement at the wrong things may seem to us to show corruption of mind, cruelty, or bad taste."[163]

Humor is... graceful.

A girl was sitting on the parkway in busy, noisy Brooklyn enjoying the lovely spring day. She called her friend who lived in Holland to say hello. Just when she finished dialing, noisy emergency vehicles clanged by with sirens screeching. Friend from Holland: "I hear the national anthem of New York..."

Isn't that a graceful way of paying homage to a noisy city?

(Just for fun, let's imagine a humorless response. They could have griped about the ubiquitous noise of the city. "I can't hear you!" "This city is so annoying.")

A pet peeve is trying to get family members to close the lights. It's a hopeless case. Try saying it this way: "Yes, the electric company sends us bills every month. You kids thought it was free, eh? But don't worry, they know we have *yichus* (illustrious lineage) so we don't have to pay ." I heard this quip from a man who claims direct lineage to the Chozeh of Lublin.[164] But there's good news: we can all cash in, because we all have lineage traced back to our forefathers. Now all we need to do is convince the utility companies.

Humor is a great way of doing business. Even the unpleasant aspect of business can be conducted more gracefully. The following example is from a debt-collection agency: *We appreciate your business, but please, give us a break. Your account is ten months overdue. That means we carried you longer than your mother did...* Compare that to the standard strident tone: If we don't receive payment in ten days, we will turn it over to a...[165]

Humor transforms niggling negatives into pleasant positives. In a preschool nursery class at the beginning of the semester, children were adjusting to separation from their mommies. An assistant in one class commented, "If their mothers would only know how often they're thought of."

Humor reassures people that we are dealing gracefully with a given situation. It makes us easier to live with. For example, instead of giving in to depression, a multiple sclerosis patient remarked, "One good thing about MS is that I don't have to worry about stirring my coffee anymore."

Humor is... a reframer

Reframing a situation makes it possible to turn a situation upside down. More accurately, it can turn an upside-down situation right-side-up — without moving a limb, merely by a sleight of words or wordless thoughts in the mind. (What an amazing exercise; even couch potatoes can enjoy this!) Nothing changed except the way we look at it.

Reframing a bad event changes a "bad" situation into a sign of good fortune, like saying "*mazel tov!*" when something breaks.

An elderly relative, may she be well, an indomitable woman who lost her husband but not her effervescent personality, made a humorous comment during a phone conversation. She laughed heartily and quoted a Russian expression that translates roughly as: "We can laugh, or we can hang [ourselves]." We are not suicidal (G-d forbid) and she apologized for the gruesome half of the idiom. What was useful was the affirmation of laughter to keep the spirits up.

"Hanging could be okay," I assured her (my reframing skills were freshly honed from my work on this chapter), "if you get the right 'hang' of it, as Reb Shmuel Munkes did."

> Reb Shmuel Munkes was a chassid of the Alter Rebbe, Reb Shneur Zalman, known for his antics. He was once discovered hanging onto the outside bars of his Rebbe's window. "What are you doing there, Reb Shmuel?" passersby asked in astonishment. "Every trade puts out a sign to show what type of establishment it is, and to advertise their wares. The shoemaker puts out a shoe, and so on. A Rebbe needs to have a chassid outside his place to show people what he produces!"

Reframing makes any weather look rosy. My son lives in Florida. "The nice thing about Miami's summer weather," he tells us, "is we don't have heat waves."

Come on down, everybody. Don't wait for "snowbirds" weather. Here is a great age reframer.

> "What is your age?" asked the judge. "Remember you are under oath."
> "Twenty-one years and some months," the woman answered.
> "How many months?" the judge persisted.
> "One hundred and eight."

Humor inserts a chuckle into the dreariest information. Suppose we are going to open a discussion about the rampant divorce rate, a painful topic. The humorous twist elicits a laugh, and sends a burst of energy to fortify us as we deal with the painful discussion.

> What is the leading cause of divorce? Marriage!

Here's an opener for another painfully widespread issue:

> What is the only thing you can't buy with money? Poverty!

Instant Relief, Instant Results

Humor and laughter are so powerful that a little goes a long way. When we have a good, hard laugh, it yields health benefits at a fraction of the time that other exercises need. Its workout is more intense and concentrated.

Humor and laughter are fast in another way as well: Try to change "big-deal thinking." It could take years. Take the shortcut. You laugh a little, cheer your system up, and poof, it's not an issue any more. We've loosened up.

Jumping for joy is good exercise.

It's hard to see our bad-mood behavior objectively. It's easier to see its effects when we're the audience. Estie, a cute three-year-old in a kindergarten class, was a great model. She arrived in a crabby mood one morning (her mother sent along a note warning that she woke up "on the left side"). Everything was an issue. The plate was too far, someone breathed on her, she didn't have a chair. A teacher sat down near her and cheered her up with some wacky humor and laughter and her mood-level turned right-side-up soon afterward.

A crabby adult churns out chunks and shards of that same behavior, slightly dressed up in adult clothing. We overreact, exaggerate, and negatively interpret everything in our path. We notice every blemish (while life is not perfect, blemishes on bad days are unpardonable). Here's a sample commentary of a cranky mind:

Someone got ahead of me in the checkout line (*What a nerve, he should be charged with assault. And now I'll be late coming home.*) Now the bus is late as well. (*I'll end up in the doctor's office from waiting out here in this nasty weather.*)

Later that evening... Where's my husband? He said he'll be home in five minutes, twenty minutes ago. (*How did I get stuck with a man that's always late?*) He's treating me to go out for dinner, you know, (*and it's about time. I'm overworked and under-appreciated.*) That must be him on the phone... "I'll be ready in five minutes, dear."

As I give myself a last minute look-over in the mirror, I notice a new pimple on my chin. (*Oh, my face looks horrible. That pimple will ruin my entire evening!*)

Just as I am getting my coat on, half a container of milk spills on the floor (or so it seems). (*Why did the milk have to spill just now? Oy, the place is a wreck! What a way to leave a house. Maybe I should reconsider. And I have to bend down to wipe it up just when I have a pain in my side. It may just be appendicitis…*)

> *Little Effie was in his Hebrew class and was learning all about how G-d created everything, including humans. He was especially intent when his teacher got to the bit about how Eve was created out of one of Adam's ribs. Later that day, Effie's mother noticed him lying on the couch. "Effie, darling, what's the matter with you?" Effie replied, "I have a pain in my side, Mommy. I think I'm going to have a wife."*

Sometimes we "have a cow" when a calf would do (we make a mountain out of a molehill) and what a waste of energy.

Two humor strategies we can always fall back on: *change-the-frame* (reframe) and *minimize-the-size.* (A nap or cup of coffee could help too.)

And if we're not up for joking, skip the joke and just cut to the laughter. It can instantly transform our mood.

Instead of having a cow, see how Reb Yankel handled the horn of a cow (actually it was the horn of a ram, but to us city dwellers, they're all the same):

> *Rosh Hashanah was approaching and Reb Yankel took out the shofar to practice. The shofar could be a quirky instrument, and Reb Yankel couldn't get good sound out of it. He got red in the face while the shofar barely squawked. Reb Yankel stopped to catch his breath and laughed. The laughter discharged the tension. And the shofar blew like a dream, and like never before. The laughter had wrought instant relief — and instant results.*

And now, back to that kindergarten class: Notwithstanding Estie's grumpy mood, children are our great modelers of buoyant spirits.

The children are standing in a circle, waiting eagerly for their favorite music-and-movement song to begin. The teacher inserts the wrong CD, then another, and then gives up, "Children, I can't find the right CD." I noticed that most of the children laughed at the difficulty — I knew I could count on children!

Here are some ways to "humorize" big-deal thinking:

1. Change a word: Instead of big *deals*, look for big *jokes*. Life is full of them.
2. Change the intonation (thoughts have intonations too) from an irked-this-is-a-big-deal to a dismissive-big-deal-shrug. So he got ahead of me on the checkout line...*One never knows who's really ahead in life. Isn't the stock market the perfect proof of that?* So the milk spilled... *As the old wisdom goes, don't cry over spilt milk. Don't cry — laugh!* So your husband is a little late... (*Recent tests proved a woman's "I'll be ready in five minutes" and a man's "I'll be home in five minutes" last exactly the same amount of time.*)

   I guarantee you will see a new you next time you look in the mirror, pimple or not.
3. Play the "change" game (see chapter 13).

   Many times when I'm feeling harassed by all the items on my to-do list, I have to stop and remind myself: Enjoy the process! No fun waiting till it's over...

   And you know what? Humor, even when there's no crisis, does make life more enjoyable.

   Would someone please mail me a reminder once in a while?

Dr. Ed Yisroel Susskind, Ph.D., clinical psychologist, lists some good reasons to use humor:[166]

It generates a congenial atmosphere. "Laughter is the fastest way to connect hearts." "You" and "I" becomes "us."

It's a gentler way of introducing a truth. "Many a truth may be told in jest," wrote Geoffrey Chaucer. Humor penetrates past our defenses.

Humor literally changes our brain chemistry and makes us more receptive to creating new neural connections.

It can turn a negative (historic) association into a source of joined laughter. A key word or phrase provides a shared vocabulary. For example, the word *Pinocchio* was used, a few decades back, to remind kids to stick to the truth. (Where did that popular association go? I hope it didn't disappear with the truth.)

Here's a great story about "shared vocabulary":

I needed someone to run out and pick up my fish order so I could get the fish up and cooking for Sukkos (we used to mix our own gefilte fish in those days). My son Avremi could pick it up on his way back from morning minyan, but he was on vacation schedule. I called him on the intercom to his room, "Avremi! Avremi! I need you to pick up the fish… Avremi, Avremi, wake up!" Moments later, a guest who was staying at our house, Rabbi Avrohom, was in the kitchen. "Do you need me to pick something up for you?" How mortified I was! I had forgotten that my son had moved out of his room to accommodate our guest.

The line became a shared joke that we recalled laughingly when Rabbi Avrohom would visit from out-of-town. That was to the credit of Rabbi Avrohom — a man with a twinkle in his eye. The predisposition to humor helped both of us file it away in our memory banks as a humorous event.

Years later, when Rabbi Avrohom was hospitalized and in failing health, his daughter put the phone to his ear though he was weak and somewhat disoriented. I said jocularly, "Hello, Avremi, could you go pick up the fish?" His daughter reported that his face lit up with the broadest smile she had seen in quite some time. "His face just shone" she said with delight, thanking me for the burst of cheer.

The humor took root because he lived each day ready and waiting for something to laugh about and it yielded its rich fruit years later when the soul craved nourishment.

And the list goes on:

- Humor helps us see the situation from a higher vantage point, to rise above, to let go, to see a different angle (maybe humor could be useful in geometry class?). It creates mental distance.
- Humor heightens tolerance for irritating issues and people (either they are, or our interpretation is making it so).
- Humor helps recovery from a mishap.
- Humor saves face or rescues us from a sticky situation.
- Humor breaks the grip of a tense situation; it softens conflicts.
- Humor acts as an antidote (an antacid substitute?) to anger or disappointment, or being slighted or told off. Things don't feel as bad or painful or scary when you can look at them through the prism of a joke.

"A measure of levity helps to preserve our sanity."[167] Sanity…what a handy quality. The more humor we get out there, the more sane people there will be around to agree.

-12-

Joy Co-conspirators: Humor and Laughter

'm sure we have noticed by now that laughter and humor are quite enmeshed. It's hard to disengage the two from each other. What came first, the chicken or the egg? Did laughter produce joy or was joy the starter? Or maybe a spark of humor fertilized it all into existence and got the ball — and the people — rolling?

After G-d created the world, He created man and woman. And then to keep the whole thing from collapsing, He created humor.

And laughter obviously erupted in the wake of the first punch line:

> A doctor and lawyer were discussing who came first. The doctor said, "It was the doctor; as we see G-d did surgery on Adam and created Eve." "No, it was the lawyer." "How do you know?" "Well, who do you think made the chaos?"

On what day was humor created? Some say on the day color was created (source unknown).[168] (Everything was black and white, until...)

Can you imagine life without humor and laughter? It would be a world robbed of its colors, a bleak business-like existence moving glumly along in black and white.

Another opinion is: humor was created the first time a Jew found himself in a mess. And truly, humor's popularity rating soared in direct correlation to the *tzores*, but I prefer to see it as a Divine gift of kindness to help us get through the *galus* challenges. Let's thank G-d for having created the possibility to reframe our challenges into absurd forms with user-friendly handles!

Humor makes the leap from surviving to thriving.

Whatever the case, once there is a chicken, expect more eggs.

Laughing at a funny line can yield two benefits. The joke is enjoyed for its own sake, and then there is an independent value in laughter that lightens our lives and takes us momentarily outside ourselves. Researchers aren't sure if it's actually the act of laughing that makes people feel better. A good sense of humor, a positive attitude, and the support of friends and family might play a role, too.[169]

(And don't waste time wondering which of the two is superior, more durable or deeper. They are not in competition with each other. Only unhappy people feel the need to compete. These two creations want only to give, to boost each other, and to bring joy and well-being to G-d's world.)

A man in the city of Dantzig had fallen into a river. He was struggling and his strength was ebbing. Reb Simcha Bunim of Pshische, who was in the city at the time, realized that there was no way this man could be rescued. The only hope was to somehow help the drowning person shore up new hope and with it renewed powers. With a hint of smile, Reb Bunim called out to him, "Send my regards to the Leviathan!"[170] What an inopportune time to crack a joke! But the tzadik knew what he was doing. Somehow the humor of that comment with the little crumb of joy it contained provided a new surge of strength for the drowning man, and miraculously he was able to remain above the water and survive.

Can we tease apart whether it was the humor, the joy or a spark of laughter that fortified the struggling man? All we need to know is that when we're "in the deep end," joking and laughing about painful things helps us rebound.

The fact that the laughter response center in the brain is in direct proximity to the fear and pain centers tells us that one "button" may cover for others. When faced with a "fight or flight" dilemma, we can flee, fight, or make a humorous remark. Cracking a joke is a better way to live than cracking up. We still "crack up" but everyone is welcome to join.

From here on, we will enjoy humor and laughter side by side. The two buddies have pledged to stick together through thick and thin. *Laughter & Humor, Inc!*

-13-

The Marketplace

*R*av Baroka was surveying the scene in a marketplace, together with the prophet Elijah. He asked the prophet, "Who in this marketplace is deemed deserving of Olam Haba (the World to Come)?" Unfortunately, Elijah saw no one that fit the bill. Soon, two people wandered in, and Elijah pointed them out saying, "These two are assured a place in the World to Come." They seemed quite ordinary, so Rav Baroka, curious to hear what they did to earn this remarkable promised reward, questioned them. "We are comedians," they told him. They related that, in addition to livening people up with their jokes, they would cheer up people who had quarreled. When the parties were cheerier, it was easier to make peace among them.[171]

Who's going to Olam Haba?

I thanked a relative for e-mailing a few of his favorite jokes. He had subsequently excused himself for not having time to send more. "You already bought Olam Haba. Your few jokes went a long way," I assured him.

He wrote back: Did you mean, they went a lo-o-n-g way all the way to Olam Haba...? I don't mind if you send my jokes to Olam Haba... but please don't send me... I still have time...."

What training and titles did the jesters have? How many framed certificates adorned their office walls? What sophisticated strategies and psychology theories did they use? None. They were naturally endowed entertainers (or maybe they read a book like this and trained themselves!); comedians who told jokes and made people laugh!

Humor and laughter vouchsafed these two people a coveted assurance of immediate entry into *Gan Eden*. Humor and laughter are elevated and sophisticated... when used with the right intentions.

This story piques the imagination. Eliyahu (the Hebrew form of his name) was not alive at the time that Rav Baroka lived; he lived during the time of the Kings, while Rav Baroka was a sage in a later period. However, highly elevated individuals would merit the revelation of Eliyahu. I would think Rab Baroka would have utilized every moment to help solve unanswered Torah mysteries and riddles, or burning contemporary dilemmas.

And here they are, looking around, "surveying the market," like the marketing analysts of today. What are the "going" items? What commodity will be found to be noteworthy and of value?

Comedy turned out to be a winner. Then and now... the more things change, the more they stay the same! Joyous Jewish living is indeed a burning contemporary issue.

The market of today — life — is a lively scene. Perhaps Eliyahu is surveying our market as well, assessing the current trends... looking for those who deserve the World to Come (as the days of Moshiach are called[172]) by bringing joy to people. (An apt analogy: consumer activity in Jewish communities is at its peak on *erev Shabbos*, corresponding to our current time.)

Hmm... Eliyahu is the one who will come to inform us the Redemption is nigh (three days prior, according to some opinions). Is this part of the Divine puzzle we've stumbled on? An intriguing thought...

In the upcoming section, we offer samples of the joy producers of today, disseminating the much-needed commodities of humor, laughter, and joy to help us survive the challenging climate of our own time.

The more joy, the merrier. The more joy produced, the faster we leap into a state of permanent joy. (G-d responds to our initiative; when we're joyous it elicits His joy.)

Laughter Specialists

Laughter Improv Fosters Home Improv-ment with Sarah Tikvah

A director, a creative producer, and a few players are ready and willing to resurrect your sense of laughter and delight. They use no costumes, just creative imagination to come up with charming scenes and good healthy laughter. And best of all, the acts translate into real life skills that make your life better than ever.

Sarah Tikvah Kornbluth, the producer, generally comes up with the creative germ, which is then presented by her troupe of players. Attendees in the audience often join the acts. Participants are encouraged to offer suggestions about stressful situations that are spontaneously incorporated into the act.

In addition to the scenes and episodes, they have an array of great games. One game is "Sing It." A crisis situation is presented. Participants are asked to flesh it out by quickly naming a location and/or suggesting the characters. As they are playing out an altercation, someone in the audience calls out, "Stop – sing it!" They then break out in song using the last line as its lyrics.

This could easily be transposed to our lives. Laughing about things that are getting us angry could salvage the situation. Suppose someone in the house is working up a temper and getting mad. Before a storm could erupt, or before the vituperation gets out of hand, quick! — "laugh-sing" the last line that was flung into the air. It works magic to cool down the simmering tempers.

Another game is "Props." In this activity you make nothing out of something by making something out of nothing. A cut-up pile of yarn, for example, could be your ruined *sheitel* (wig), a new head fashion to cover bald spots, or a make-your-own-mattress kit (it's beginning to look like psychoanalysis of our personal wish-lists).

We could apply out-of-the-box thinking such as non-toothbrush uses for the toothbrush, but better yet is to assign meaning to random unidentifiable items (recycled from the pile of clutter with which homes are amply blessed), the more preposterous the better. How therapeutic it is to laugh away our familiar disasters.

Would you like anything changed in your house? "Change!" is a must-play game. Two players are assigned associated roles such as a dentist and a patient, a wife and a mother-in-law, a tourist guide and tourist. A crisis is described. For example, the tourist guide and tourist are lost. The guide declares, "I've been doing this for thirty years and this never happened to me." A person (pre-assigned) calls out "Change!" The tourist guide offers a revised statement, such as, "I started yesterday and it never happened to me." "Change!" she says, once again. "I've been doing this for a while, but somehow it always happens to me!"

A member of her troupe played "Change!" with her own family — in "real time." Her son asked for a ridiculously large amount of money for a party he wanted to make with his friends. *This is getting out of hand*, she thought. "Change!" she called out. He asked for a lesser amount, and it was approved. But then her kids played it on her. No one was eating the supper she had managed to prepare on a stressful day. "This supper is delicious and you will eat it if I have to force it down your throats." "Change!" her son sang out. "Okay, you don't like it, but I'm still making you eat it. "Change!" "Okay, go find something else that appeals to you." (Get to the fridge fast everyone, before mom changes her mind!) This exercise does wonders to stop rising anger in its tracks.

Wouldn't it be nice to change our default way of speaking to children, spouses, clients, students from "no!" to "yes!"? Naturally we'd rather be saying "yes" more often, but children have a knack of painting us into corners. Learn "the art of the ridiculous." When the child says, "Could I have another candy?" you respond with "Yes! You can have fourteen candies (shock...), and you can also have fourteen cavities, two stomachaches, and as many trips to the doctor as you like..." Humor can achieve far more than anger!

Couldn't we all benefit from "home-improv-ment"? They say the biggest room in the house is the room for improvement.

Participants at laughter-improv events gain new ways to approach the tired and familiar aspects of their lives. They have learned to see things that make them seriously irritated, seriously agitated, seriously frustrated, in a more playful way.

They have been helped to un-irritate, un-agitate, un-frustrate, and take life in stride. Does everyone like themselves better for it? YES![173]

Discover Your Inner Laughter with Esther Rachel

Did you ever wish you could be in two places at once?

I was participating in a workshop at a women's convention. In the room next to ours, Esther Rachel Russell was running a workshop on laughter: improvisation and learning how to arouse one's inner laughter. The uproarious laughter coming through the wall made me wish I could be there. But I also wanted to participate in the workshop in which I had taken my seat as my daughter-in-law was giving a fascinating presentation on quick and easy fine-dining ideas. Good food beautifully presented does increase joy, as all the cookbook names out there will testify. However, they won't make you laugh (unless you try adding some - fill in the blank here - to your recipe. C'mon, pros, let's have some humor improv!), and in any case, laughing with a mouth full of food is dangerous.

Esther Rachel explained how the humor works its magic. The process of transforming issues to comic form separates the person from the stressor. We are on one side; the problem is on the other side. By effecting that separation, we've disempowered its power.

Participants choose a characteristic within themselves that they wish to transform. They get up and do a vignette with another person that accentuates and exaggerates that negative characteristic. It is a form of parody, and it serves to transform that negative trait into levity. The parody and laughter allows the person to view it from a distance. That space is therapeutic; it is where healing happens.

Laughing at oneself is very healing: "Don't be so full of yourself and your ego" it tells us. That's what comedians do — they poke fun at weaknesses.

Let's say a woman wants to improve her nervousness. She gets up and begins to exaggerate her nervousness. Everyone laughs, herself included. She is gaining control over it by magnifying it, and now she could see it in all its nervous glory. When she magnifies it, it loses potency, like when you stretch a bright red balloon and the color fades into a softer pink.

Doing "Joy-Breaks-Through" exercises allows people to cut through all the façades and personas that they create in the world, and to access that authentic, organic part of themselves that they don't usually express. Once you break one barrier, it opens you up to the realization that you could break other barriers and you can become something bigger and better than you ever thought you could be.[174]

Esther Rachel is covering lots of ground these days. She has branched out from a laughter improvisation leader to a worldwide presenter crisscrossing the globe and doing presentations for corporate business teams. Apparently more and more are discovering the magic of joy and laughter. She helps pinpoint pain points, reframe perceptions and shake up their status quo. "The workshop 'Joy Breaks Barriers' was more than amazing," reports a participant. "Not only did it help the staff loosen up and laugh together, it also helped the staff recognize that if we can find joy and laughter in the things that we do every day, then we can find healing in the most curious of places."

The Life of a Clown: Avraham Landau

Let's get a view from inside the costume. [175] Avraham Landau was a clown first and a religious Jew second. What turned him on? Guess? It was a Purim experience. He wasn't sure clowning and religion were compatible, but his rabbi assured him that bringing joy to people would bring salvation, relief, and growth. He has seen all these come true in his work.

Everything was going well. Then he decided to move to Israel.

"Nobody in Israel believed me when I told them what I did for a living; people thought I was teasing them until I started carrying my clown suit around with me." Avraham had made *aliyah* to a country that did not list clowns as a career option.

A few months after arriving in Israel, he received his draft notice. He reported to his local recruitment office. "Profession?" the officer asked.

"Clown!"

The officer was so enraged that he considered arresting him for his insolence. Avraham showed the officer his official diploma but he was still not convinced that clowning was an actual profession. He was told to return in a week.

One week later, Avraham was back in the recruitment center at the end of a long, long line. After a while, to relieve his boredom, he slipped on his clown suit and started doing a jig. Like magic, the place came alive. Soldiers and recruits started clapping their hands and laughing. The commanding officer came out of his office to see what caused the commotion.

"Okay!" he yelled at me. "Go home. You've proved your point."

Avraham still serves, though. He travels the country to boost the morale of soldiers who are serving and fighting from their desolate posts.

Of course, children are his main fans, but he has to deal with the fear of the little ones (those under age three) as well. For them he tones down his act and makeup. "And then we all have a wonderful time. It's a rush of pure, innocent joy that's more meaningful to me than any amount of money."

Although most people love to laugh, Avraham has seen plenty of misery. At an old-age home, he noticed a resident in the crowd with "one of the saddest expressions I'd ever seen." It just broke his heart. He learned that this man had suffered greatly in life. Our erstwhile clown was determined not to leave the place until he would see the man laugh. Not a little smirk, but a genuine belly laugh, an all-out guffaw. It wasn't easy.

The man ignored me completely and even looked rather impatient, eager for the performance to be over. But I would not let up. I used every ounce of energy and every single technique in the book until he finally cracked.

His laughter was pure music to my ears. It was undoubtedly the pinnacle of my career: I had made a truly miserable man happy. I told the staff that I would come again the next day and the next, until the poor man learned how to smile by himself. But man plans and G-d laughs...

The following day I arrived at the nursing home raring to go, but I didn't find the man in his room or in the dining room. I went to the nurses' station to inquire. Their expressions told me everything I needed to know. The man had passed away in the middle of the night.

I joined the few mourners following his casket to pay my final respects. Silently I whispered, "My dear friend, whose name I don't even know, I very much wanted to bring another smile to your face, but G-d willed otherwise. I thank Him that I was able to do it at least once and that you experienced some measure of joy, albeit on your very last day. Rest in peace."

Comedy Cures with Sara Chana

As a newly diagnosed cancer patient with a dismal prognosis back in 1999, Saranne (as she was then known) Rothberg decided to pursue her own healing. She was inspired by the writings of Norman Cousins, a pioneer in holistic healing. By Divine Providence, she had come across an excerpt of his book in which he describes how he overcame illness with humor and laughter.

As soon as she was diagnosed with cancer, she went out and rented every comedy tape she could find, put her only daughter to bed and inserted the first video. Problem was that she was sobbing so hard she couldn't even hear the punch lines. She forced herself to persevere, watching video after video until slowly she got into the comedy spirit and actually began to laugh. Next morning, she appointed her daughter to be her "humor buddy" and made a daily "appointment to laugh." She pledged to find joy and celebrate their blessings every day.

At her first chemotherapy treatment, she threw a "celebration of life party" and included everyone there, including the medical staff. She came armed with six hours worth of comedy reel, party favors, and desserts. Skepticism turned to laughter as the positive energy pervaded the room. "It was hard to tell who was the patient and who was the nurse; the lines were blurred. There was so much positive energy. Everyone was having fun."[176]

Right there in the cancer trenches, during that first treatment, her vision was born. Saranne had discovered her mission. She would bring light, happiness, and hope into the darkest of places. She launched the organization called Comedy Cures and ran it from her chemo chair. It was a chair she occupied through three surgeries, forty-four radiation treatments, and two-and-a-half years of intense chemotherapy — three times a day at one point.

Today, Saranne is a stage IV cancer survivor and a world-renowned mind/body and therapeutic laughter expert. When I first met her, possibly a decade ago, she was gradually drawing closer to the commitments of a Torah life. Today she calls herself Sara Chana, and says that while it was G-d that cured her, the laughter and comedy therapy provided tools that G-d had placed in our natures. Her joyful spirit provided emotional strength so that her physical body could withstand the years of grueling treatments, while spiritually it helped her maintain her faith.

Sara Chana is a woman with a single-minded goal: to help you find joy in your journey. The Comedy Cures Foundation tickles funny bones. They bring joy, laughter, and therapeutic humor programs to kids and grown-ups living with illness, depression, trauma, and disabilities.[177]

The Joy-Power of Posing-as-If

To introduce the next laughter specialist, we will first study the power of using our physical means to affect our emotional outlook.

You've been out of a job for months, and you're going for an interview.

You're taking a test that is very important to your future, as well as your immediate life.

You need a driver's license — now.

Many people get so nervous when they have to perform that they undermine their chances for success. Others are simply shy. One doesn't have to say a word at the interview. Nonverbal body language could affect the outcome, whether you will win or lose the moment's objective.

Nervousness and shyness are not merely abstract emotions. They bring about physical changes in our bodies by releasing hormones and other chemicals that affect our brain. Cortisol is produced by stress. The way students sit in class — assertive and confident positions, or not — are clear indicators of their cortisol levels, as testing showed. We know that we could use our minds to change our bodies, but can our bodies change our minds?

Our hearts are drawn in the direction of our external activity, say our wise rabbis.[178] "If you want a quality, act as if you already had it."[179] That's a shout-out from William James, pioneer of American psychology. We know he didn't originate the idea, but he deserves our pat-on-the-back for championing it.

Dr. Amy Cuddy, a social psychologist, has done extensive research in this area. She knew that high power "alpha type" personalities affect others, but she wondered: do our actions affect our own selves?[180]

Her conclusions: your body language shapes who you are.

An erect bearing, as we know, projects an image of self-confidence. This perceived self-assurance often carries the person into genuine confidence. That positive feedback becomes self-perpetuating: When people believe that you are secure, they will treat you that way, which helps you further boost your self-esteem.

Body language affects how others see us, but it may also change how we see ourselves. We can make immediate changes in our body chemistry simply by changing body positions.

When Dr. Cuddy taught an insecure student to adopt a leadership pose, the chemicals in her brain changed correspondingly. All students needed were two minutes of power-posing (in some unobtrusive area). Their stress levels reduced, their assertiveness hormone went up — and their performance levels with it.

If you're wondering about the scientific underpinnings, here's what's involved: "Power posing" raises testosterone levels in the brain. A higher level of this hormone causes people to feel assertive and confident. At the same time, it lowers cortisol levels in the brain, which is good, because cortisol is a stress hormone that makes a person anxious and impedes clear decision-making.

How do we power pose? High-power poses are body positions that expand the space your body takes up. Some examples: when sitting, lean back in a chair with feet and hands as expansive as possible; when standing, do so with feet planted widely apart, or if standing at a table, lean forward on a table with arms and hands solidly planted on table. Low-power poses include scrunched up shoulders and positions such as crossing your hands and ankles, taking up the least space possible. The weakest power pose is resting your hands on your neck, a pose redolent with uncertainty and anxiety.

"V for victory" is a famous pose that communicates the confidence of a person who just won a physical competition. Holding a V-hands-up position with widened leg stance for two minutes in a private area such as a stairwell will invest your upcoming performance with confidence.

Do it, even if it's hard for you, Dr. Cuddy advises, though you feel it's killing you with the difficulty of it, though you feel like a fake and a fraud.

> *Rabbi DovBer of Lubavitch wrote a letter responding to a person whose son had died. The father was grief-stricken and found it difficult to return to his "old self." In the letter, the Rebbe told the father that he must serve G-d with happiness, and "If you are not happy inwardly, that at least do something joyous outwardly."* (Power smile, power pose, power laugh, power sing, power dance...)

This is not the "fake it till you make it" that grows on a person gradually. These are real chemical changes that set immediate emotional changes into motion.

Back to Laughter...

For those days when you're simply not in the mood... the same concept applies.

- Mike is in no mood for jokes. His employer called him in today and notified him that he's cutting his overhead expenses and will be dismissing some employees. His position there is clearly in jeopardy. Stress begins to course through his system.
- Myrna's been through a harrowing few weeks with her mother in and out of the hospital. She just found out her mother was readmitted. Her throat went dry with dread.
- Devorah just got off the phone with her housekeeper-babysitter who called to tell her she was quitting. Devorah's stomach landed somewhere between her knees. How would she manage her multiple duties, including her teaching job?

Mike, Myrna, and Devorah are just not in the humorous frame of mind; it would be almost callous to cheer them up with a joke right now. Being in a joyful state makes it easier to be optimistic, to see that there may be a sunny side to the situation now or later. But how can we find joy when we're drowning in misery? (Did you ever try to find your glasses when you're not wearing them? When your vision is compromised, it's that much harder to locate them — you glasses-wearers will know what I mean.)

Help! Are there comedians on call tonight? Any funny shows on the calendar? That humorist I watched last night was good, but the humor wasn't *mine*. Although I'm getting mileage out of it, it's an external crutch that is not always available. That's why learning how to generate our *own* laughter comes in handy.

Let the comedians stay home... We have good news! While we are not all born with humor, we were all born with the laughter reflex. Everyone can laugh. Laughter workshops are where *you* make it happen; where you create your own laughs.

Laughter workshops offer an exciting shortcut, something unique to our times, a new way to laugh and gain control over your life and health as well. It has been tried and proven by people around the world. If you think power poses pack power, wait till you try this brand of laughter, also known as "mechanical laughter."

Laughter is the tech-age medicine and preventive treatment for both body and soul. And what's nice, laughter is a cheap and efficient medicine. This reflex that we are born with, that precedes many illnesses that beset people, may be a case of the "cure preceding the malady," because it holds the key to good health. As with power poses, we will see that real chemical changes take place that set physical and emotional changes in motion.

Get ready to laugh Mike, Myrna, Devorah, and all you others. Now. No joke. Right, no jokes needed. No sense of humor. This is "No-Joke-Laughter."

You can run out of jokes, but laughter is a replenishable resource.

The Laughter Ambassador — Tzipi Dagan

One day, I got a most unusual invitation in the mail. They say there's nothing new in the world, but this invitation was definitely stranger than a moon rock to me: "You are invited to an event — the Gift of Laughter," it read, presented by a Certified Laughter Instructor.

The concept of a laughter workshop was new to me. Who would guess that there are 6,000 clubs worldwide, and fifty in Israel alone!

G-d put this wonderful laughing reflex into our systems. You'd think that laughing should come naturally to people. It does, initially; children don't need much reason to laugh. But little by little, life's serious side intrudes and erodes our spirits. If we adults would all laugh a little more, life would be so much happier.

"That is precisely why we *should* be laughing!" says Tzipi Dagan, who came to the U.S. from Israel on a tour. "The more issues and difficulties in a person's life, the more important it is to laugh. Laughter releases special endorphins that cleanse a person, and give them a boost. A good laugh is similar to the effect of a good cry, but so much healthier! No matter what's going on in your life, there's always something to laugh about."

Remember the way we used to dare our friends when we were kids: "Try to make me laugh!" Only those with Herculean control could contain the gales of laughter from bursting forth. Try to make me laugh now! It gets harder as we get older. No wonder every person I told about the upcoming laughter workshop had the same response: Will she have lots of good jokes? Is she a comedian of good repute? That's the only way we adults expect to laugh.

I was concerned; will the humor be good enough to help people who are in serious crises, who really need the cheering up? As for me, I only laugh at *very* funny jokes, and I was pretty sure I would be nothing more than a curious spectator. Still, my curiosity was aroused.

As it turned out, Tzipi's workshop was not a ha ha–event where someone rolls out jokes and the audience chuckles in appreciation. It is truly a workshop in the sense that everyone is an active participant in generating laughter for a healthy lifestyle — to help us regain a fuller quality of joy in our lives.

Before launching into the actual exercises, the audience watches some video clips to loosen up (as well as some breathing and light movement for warm-ups). As we see groups of women from all currents of Judaism chortling away, our inhibitions fade away and we begin to believe that it is possible to laugh unabashedly. Laughter is definitely contagious.

Here's how the workshop "works": Guided laughter is interspersed with periods of deep breathing and exercises to open constricted muscles and bring oxygen to every part of the body.

The workshop intersperses laughter with deep breathing exercises, music, and fun motions. There are exercises that engage those who are as yet unaccustomed to laugh. Guided aerobic free-form movements loosen up stiff muscles while facilitating release of tensions and giving free expression to one's inner feelings. (Power poses are embedded throughout the session!) One wonders if it's really possible to coax people to get "out-of-their-box." Tzipi doesn't seem to have a problem with that. She gets everyone to laugh. "At first it's a mechanical, forced laughter, but participants get into the mood soon enough." The laughter session teaches us to activate our laughter reflex, consciously and willfully. We learn to train the laughter muscles so we can activate them deliberately at will. "I teach the women how to laugh. It's an art," she explains. These exercises should be practiced regularly, like any aerobics exercise class.

Laughter gains power when people practice it together. "There's something so liberating about laughing together, a sidesplitting laughter for no other reason than that we're together, enjoying each other's company and shedding stress. The larger the group, the more laughter will be generated. Imagine the scene of twenty or thirty women holding their sides and laughing together. It sounds simplistic, but it's so healing."

How about two or three hundred women in a room tingling with laughter!

How did no-joke laughter start? A doctor from India, Dr. Kataria, now world-renowned, had made an exciting discovery: the brain does not differentiate between real laughter and mechanical laughter. Health benefits are the same in both cases. The discovery provided the momentum for worldwide laughter clubs.

Tzipi took Dr. Kataria's course when he visited Israel. She tried it on her family, then with some friends, and then started an unofficial "laughter club." At first, it was greeted with skepticism. "People thought it was a bunch of hocus-pocus, something like a clown show," but those who attended were instantly hooked.

"There is nothing miraculous or magical about these groups. It's just common sense. Learning how to laugh, how to loosen up your muscles and breathe deeply, to find the humor in everything, literally prolongs your life."

These external actions have a real impact on the internal state of mind and on one's attitude.[181] Eventually we get hooked and become sincere participants. There are exercises for anger, fear, and worry, as well. When these negative emotional responses are eliminated, the calmer state leads naturally to an improvement in social interactions, spousal and otherwise.

I tried one of the exercises to help with my little granddaughter's fears. I helped her grab that fear in a neat little charade and evict it

Tzipi has adapted laughter yoga to the ideals of Torah and woven them into the fabric of her sessions. She is steering us towards the ultimate "our mouths will be filled with laughter" — pure laughter, no jokes needed. Her workshops are approved, even recommended, by many Orthodox rabbis in Israel. She runs training programs so that more and more ambassadors will be bringing health, healing, and the ability to serve G-d with joy to more and more people.[182]

Laughter clubs are helping many strands of needs: People who are overweight due to "emotional eating" (inner stress), helping seniors stay in shape, and people suffering from depression. Sample videos are available online to give people an idea of how the clubs weave their magical healing wand. Laughter therapy is recommended for singles, couples, families, and children.

Laughter Drums

Malky Levine has combined laughter and drums to form "Laughter Drumming." In Drums Alive, laughter, rhythm, and energy are all drum-rolled in one. I watched a clip and noticed that the elaborate drum-strokes share common characteristics with the power-poses that inspire confidence and leadership. Maybe we could dub this winning combination "power-poses-plus."

Participants in a "Drums Alive" session get a real charge. "I felt more alive after a session than I've felt in years." Another was "high" from the high-powered body-soul-emotional recharge.

And meet the family: You can join Malky's sister Esther Rotenberg for a session with shakers and tap dancing if you're looking for an elegant energy and want to "move."

Or you can join their mother Rebbetzin Aidel Miller, who has made it her mission to uplift people with laughter, drums, and one-of-a-kind stories.

Why don't we just call them "the Laughter Family?"

Section IV
Mind-Body Connection

-14-

De-stress the Stress

All the world is but a stage. So much for the world. We, the players, sometimes feel like we're garbed and costumed in pressure suits that constrict us with tight rubber bands of drama, stress, conflicts, high, and low moments. One way we can not only survive — but thrive — is to break the grip of life's dramas through humor and laughter.

Stress is like a balloon. Too often in life, stress builds up, swelling up somewhere in our innards. Suddenly a joke, and pop — the stress balloon bursts, and its trapped energy is free to circulate once again in confluence with its environment. Some say laughter is an escape — escaping the bad energy of an event. Knowing how to be jolly and occasionally silly can help deflect escalating tensions, even potentially violent situations.

The correlation between our emotional state and our physical health has become an accepted fact:[183] "Feelings are chemical: They can kill or cure!"[184]

Writer Norman Cousins[185] was almost paralyzed with an agonizing and supposedly incurable disease. Despite his doctor's gloomy prognosis, Cousins was determined to cure himself through laughter. And so he sat in bed and read funny stories, joke books, anything to make him laugh. He soon recovered, to the astonishment of his medical team.

In his popular book *Anatomy of an Illness*,[186] he describes an outpouring of support for his premise that "no medication... was as potent as the state of mind that a patient brings to his or her own illness."[187]

The term psychoneuroimmunology, coined in 1975, refers to the study of the mind-body relationship, in particular the effects of stress on the immune system. Mind-body science has been snowballing ever since.

Stress hormones have a bad reputation; and are usually vilified as "the bad guys." The relationship between stress (negative emotions) and disease and illness is profound. It is believed that 80 to 90 percent of all disease is stress related.[188] Familiar examples are back pain, ulcers and other stomach woes, and heart conditions, but the impact of stress is far greater.

It's not all bad though! Though stress is known to have a deleterious effect, there is also a good kind of stress. *Eustress* is a name for the good stress ("eu" from the Greek word meaning *well* or *good*). Eustress is created when you take on a challenge that you welcome. *Distress* is the result of negative perceptions associated with an event.

If you approach a task with hope and vigor, and think you'll derive vigor and meaning from it, you've just imbibed eustress. The body itself cannot physically discern between the two. It is the mind that decides. If we don't want to life to disarm us, we'll have to learn how to disarm stress. The trick is to either shift our perspective, or knock it out before it gets us. Call in Humor & Laughter, Inc. Laughter is magical. It simultaneously *lowers* bad stress hormones while it *raises* (and creates) good stress hormones.

Stress weighing a thousand pounds is stubbornly lodged in my innards.[189]

The benefits of eustress:

Laughter is a tranquilizer with no side effects.[190]

- *Increases* natural killer cells that attack viruses and some types of cancer and tumor cells.
- *Increases* IgB, the immunoglobulin produced in large quantities.
- *Increases* complement 3, which helps antibodies to attack dysfunctional and infected cells.
- *Increases* T-cell activity. Laughter helps these cells to "turn it up a notch."

(See more laughter and humor facts in the Health-Menu appendix.)

I-stress, eu-stress...
I scream, you scream...
let's relax with ice cream...

Rabinovich sits down in a café and orders a glass of tea and a copy of Pravda. "I'll bring the tea," the waiter tells him, "but I can't bring you a copy of Pravda. The Soviet regime has been overthrown and Pravda isn't published anymore." "All right," says Rabinovich, "just bring me the tea." The next day, Rabinovich comes to the same café and asks for tea and copy of Pravda. The waiter gives him the same answer. On the third day, the scenario repeated itself once again. This time the waiter says to him, "Look, sir, you seem to be an intelligent man. For the past three days you ordered a copy of Pravda, and three times now I've had to tell you that the Soviet regime has been overthrown, and Pravda isn't published anymore." "I know, I know," says Rabinovich. "But I just like to hear it."

Physically and mentally, humor is the opposite of stress.[191] Count on it to undo stress.[192]

In any volatile situation, when we feel ourselves getting heated up, annoyed, angry, irritated, resentful, or tense, we could go into stormy meltdowns

It is impossible for us to be angry and laugh at the same time. We have the power to choose either.

or we could serenely chill with saved-in-the-nick-of-time (humorous or other) cooldowns. Hopefully, cooldown wins, everything stabilizes, and humor, the hero, is free to go on to his next mission.

-15-

Crash Course: Humor and Laughter Therapy

ife can be serious. People think that a serious occasion must be accompanied by a solemn demeanor, that "seriousness of purpose can only be conveyed by solemnity of tone."[194] Seriousness and laughter can weave in and out of life together. As George Bernard Shaw said, "Life does not cease to be funny when people die, any more than it ceases to be serious when people laugh."

Laughter, too, is a seriously important business. (But don't be too serious about your jokes either. So your humor fell flat. You still got a lift from the effort and you get points for having gone into "funny mode.")

Comedy is simply a funny way of being serious.[193]

Our adult culture promotes a stiff upper lip. Being vulnerable, laughing, and crying may make us uncomfortable. Instead of releasing our feelings, we are taught to view our situations cerebrally and to "be in control." This inhibition can get in our way:
People who squelch laughter and emotion become increasingly rigid. Cautious, inhibited people are rarely funny, and their rigidity makes it harder to change the behavior patterns.

> Repressing emotion locks in the pain. It's necessary sometimes to feel the pain so that we are not contained by it. Laughter and humor helps us let those trapped feelings out. When we give up control, we are actually gaining control of our lives.

The Holy Temple lay in ruins. Rabbi Akiva was walking towards the Temple Mount with three colleagues. As they got there, they beheld a fox running on the site of the Holy of Holies. The three sages burst into tears and Rabbi Akiva laughed.[195] *Not because he didn't feel the pain of the destroyed Holy Temple as much as the others did. But within the horror of the destruction he pinpointed a glimmer of light; the darkness of today revealed the brightness of tomorrow. If the awful prophecy that foxes would overrun the Holy Mount had come true, the positive prophecies about the rebuilding of Jerusalem would come to pass as well. The same bleak scene that gave his companions a reason to cry gave him a reason to laugh.*

Don't take yourself too seriously! And try not to take life so seriously! If we take ourselves *too* seriously, maybe we should take ourselves to a therapist's couch, if only to pick up a few

Things can't be that bad if we can still laugh. Things may look bad but we can still laugh.

useful tips about the many uses and usefulness of therapeutic humor and laughter...

Laughter and therapy? Ha! That's laughable. How can laughter be a vital part of a healing process when the subject matter is so serious?

Humor is used by professional therapists as a healing modality. Besides being funny, humor offers handles to help tame the most serious aspects of life.

Every therapist has his bag of tricks to help people unfurl from the grip of stress, anger, guilt, annoyance and other goodies, and humor is one of them.

Humor is ideal for the nonmobile, sick, and hospitalized. Some of the therapies available today are humor therapy, clown therapy, and laughter meditation (the latter two were featured in an earlier chapter). They help to alleviate boredom, a demoralizing condition experienced by people who are stuck at home or in hospitals.

A typical adult is said to laugh about fifteen times a day, but housebound people and hospital patients' rate of daily laughs could plummet all the way down to zero laughs per day. Clowns are becoming more frequent visitors in hospitals.

Moshe Wangrofsky,[196] a psychotherapist who uses humor, has kindly shared some valuable tips that can also be imported from the therapist's "couch" to our own living room couches as we lounge and interact with our spouses and children.

Note that obviously this home-therapy is not meant to substitute for professional help when it is warranted.

Empathy. Humor has great healing potential, and packs a powerful punch if used cautiously and sensitively. The important condition, which cannot be overstated, is that it be empathic. This means the comments, sensations, and points of view of the one venting were heard and experienced by the listener.

Trust. The professional must gain the client's trust before he undertakes to use humor in healing. He gains trust by being *empathic*. Then he introduces "empathic humor" but he maintains the trust because it is respectful. "We will never laugh at a client but we could laugh at the irrationality of the ideas," a therapist reassures us. Laughter *with* people is compassionate, laughter *at* them is immoral. A counselor or layman has to be able and willing to genuinely laugh at himself and his own shortcomings as well.

Objectivity. A clinician has a great advantage: he is not emotionally charged. This will reflect in humor that originates from a genuine place and an objective desire to support the client's progress. It's more difficult for a parent or spouse to maintain an objective, calm, and genuine demeanor when we want to lobby for changes or growth in a spouse or child. Our efforts are undermined by the fact that we are often impatient, simmering, resentful, tired, overworked, and, frankly, fed up.

Caveat. People, and parents in particular, tend to underline humor with sarcasm when addressing children and spouses, well-meaning as we are. The well-meaning spouse or parent will concoct a humorous-criticism sandwich. A child who hears her mother begin the sentence with "You did such a good job clearing the floor of your room..." is unpleasantly put off by the surprise ending, "that I can now actually see how messy the rest of your room is." Trust just got lost under the rest of that mess. "You are so talented (finally, a compliment... kids are so thirsty for those compliments) to have stained up your new shirt like that."

Parents that are going to say something negative should be upfront about it. They should not present it as a subversive message. Critical-humor sandwiches create distance between spouses as well. They are so cleverly disguised that the receiver can't even put their finger on what was wrong, and why it hits them on their wrong side. (You don't like ridicule; neither do your loved ones.)

The Paradox in Humor Therapy

The nonsensical paradox is a well-known humor-crafting ingredient. A useful strategy in humor therapy is the "paradoxical technique."

Here's an example: A therapist is meeting with a family that has a chaotic life. After having established a good beginning relationship, the therapist introduces a nonsensical paradox: "Everyone in this family is normal but the family is crazy." Individuals of the family feel validated. They're normal! Generally, when this is done, the family members laugh along with the therapist at themselves as long as it is "clear" that each of them is "normal." (If they're not, this statement would be counterproductive.)[197]

Fears and Phobias...

A person who suffers from fears or phobias may run into a further compounded fear syndrome called *anticipatory anxiety*. The person's fear of certain symptoms occurring makes the feared outcome more likely. The fear is the mother of the additional fears. Examples of anticipatory fears are blushing, sweating, and stuttering.

Viktor Frankl, neurologist and psychiatrist, used "paradoxical intention" to relieve anticipatory anxiety wherein the patient makes his goal the exact opposite of his hyper-intended goal.[198]

Larry, an accountant, who has recently been suffering from profuse sweating, will be going to meet a potential new and important client. He is worried that he will be nervous and sweat so badly that he will undermine his chances of being hired. He was instructed to tell himself, in a session with his clinician, "Now try to sweat ten buckets, instead of the usual one." He actually spoke to himself. In Larry's case, the results were impressive. One session and he was free.[199]

The patient is helped to put a distance between himself and his own neurosis. He even learns to laugh at himself. Once he can do that, he may be on the way to self-management and hopefully to cure.

Some other examples of paradoxical intention:

*A person with a writer's cramp was directed to say to himself, "Now I will show you what a good scribbler I am." The cramp was gone and he kept his bookkeeping position.

*A stutterer got on a bus but had no money for the fare. He planned to win compassion of the travelers with his bad stutter. He began to stutter, but couldn't! His stuttering disability refused to cooperate.

*A woman with OCD (obsessive-compulsive disorder) was forced to stay in bed due to excessive hand-washing and compulsions. Not any more. Whenever an obsession comes to mind, she jokes about it — joking is the paradoxical intention for her condition.

*Insomniacs, try this useful strategy to help you fall asleep: Try not to!

Even suffering could have meaning as illustrated in this example:[200]

> *Once, an elderly general practitioner consulted me because of his severe depression. He could not overcome the loss of his wife who had died two years before and whom he had loved above all else. Now how could I help him? What should I tell him? I refrained from telling him anything, but instead confronted him with a question: "What would have happened,*

doctor, if you had died first, and your wife would have had to survive without you?" "Oh," he said, "for her this would have been terrible; how she would have suffered!" Whereupon I replied, "You see, doctor, such a suffering has been spared her, and it is you who have spared her this suffering; but now, you have to pay for it by surviving and mourning her." He said no word but shook my hand and calmly left the office.

Become Your Own Therapist

Dear readers, if you have never felt angry, fearful, hurt, or depressed, don't waste your time reading this part! Hmm, seems many of you have decided to stay on. That's because our minds are forever stewing with an array of fretful thoughts, most of which are said to be negative. Negative emotions are harmful. But what could we do? We have so many misfortunes to deal with.

Q: Rabinovich, what is a fortune?

A: A fortune is to live in our Socialist motherland.

Q: And what's a misfortune?

A: A misfortune is to have such a fortune.

Humor and laughter drown them out and turn misfortune into a fortune. (It's a good time to remind ourselves that G-d disguises His kindness and there's a hidden treasure — a fortune in every misfortune.)

In crises, one could respond with a meltdown or cooldown:

- Someone parked in front of your driveway, and you can't get out. You need to get to the office. Your stress levels are going up. You're not able to change the world, but you need to do something to vanquish your anger dragon.
- Poor Morris missed his train by ten seconds. It would have been less stressful to miss it by ten minutes. If only he would have left just ten seconds earlier... Punctuality is an art he

has not mastered. He is guilty and has only himself to blame. Stress, compounded by guilt, will accompany him all the way to his appointment.

• Leah went for a haircut. She warned the haircutter to trim three inches. Instead, she was barely left with a "pixie" cut. What will she do? She can't face herself in the mirror, or anyone she knows for the next month, at least.

Let's find some strategies to respond to these situations. I'll bet many of you can dig in and come up with some great tricks of your own. Uncover that hidden talent!

Funny notes: Written notes are effective, nonviolent communicators. They're great for the many daily things that make us think: *It's so annoying.* Everyone's got their list, but here's one: The kids leave the toothpaste open — every time, no matter how many times they're told — and it sits there with a squeezed-out glob drying on its end...

How about rolling a note around the toothpaste outlining how you care about your looks and how uncomfortable you feel with your runny nose? Sign it: "Love, the Toothpaste Tube."

Write positive messages and put it in your pocket or pocketbook. Hang signs in your room, around the house or on a mirror, wherever you'll keep seeing it. Rename it and tame it... Problems are gifts... Failure leads to success... The unexpected has perfect timing... Mistakes are important events.

Learn the art of being silly when needed.

Sing: Adults can sing too when life is throwing them a curveball, together with the kids

> **Rebbe Nachman of Breslov said, "It is a great mitzvah to always be happy. It is even good to do silly things in order to cheer oneself up."[201]**

and even on your own. It may seem weird and unnatural to suggest that "proper" adults sing silly songs. Still, silly beats angry, hands down. And the stress is down too. (Song as a strategy is described above in Home-improv-ment.) And of course, regular adult songs are soothing as well.

Anything works; any kids' tune that comes quickly to mind. The lyrics don't have to be award-winning.

Low mood remedy — social banter: When people's spirits slump, they often shun the very activity that will lift them out of their huff. Let's call it the power of social banter, or light talk punctuated with humor and pockets of laughter. It takes a little while for the frozen spirits to thaw out, but they are going to be affected despite themselves.

Stop, hold everything! My daughter just walked into the kitchen with the terrible news that her Smartphone fell into the water. Oh, how disheartening. I'm not sure she's ready to sing quite yet. I'll wait a little and see. (That was very sweet of G-d to help me out with examples as I was compiling the stress-related chapters. In life there's always something new to report for the stress-producing list.)

The next morning I was commiserating with her about this joy-blocker event. She responded, "These things don't faze me." I guess we don't have to sing, then.

Entry of that evening: after hours with her telephone network, pricing a replacement phone, and getting a taste of just how many ways a non-working phone could become an annoyance, it miraculously came back to life! We all sang!

Humor is a parent's best friend (especially for teenagers). Instead of "I said — you said," you're both on the same team. Children would much rather grow up in a humorous home than a plain-Jane environment. It will generate many pleasant memories to look back on. Even if the details are not remembered, the atmosphere will be.

A man won a large sum of money in a lottery. The first thing he did was to treat his family to a round-trip ticket on a space ship for a few spins in orbit. All the neighbors and extended family crowded around them when they returned, curious to hear the first reports. "So, how was the trip?" "Okay." "How was the food?" "Okay." "How was the company?" "Okay." "Everything was just okay? You don't seem to very enthusiastic." Finally, the oldest boy in the family spoke up. "Everything was okay, but there was no atmosphere!"

Lighten things up. Lighthearted people "like" life. Serious, heavy people tend to use negatives more often. Their speech is defined by "don't like," "don't do," "not good." Would you rather walk with heaviness in the heart or lightheartedness? Humor is worth its weight in gold, except that it is lightweight. Sometimes lightness has the value.

Section V

The Whats of Humor & Laughter

-16-
What Gets the Laughs Out?

So, how does laughter actually team up with humor?

Laughter is, simply, a reflex — but not simply so. It is in a different category from other reflexes, such as blinking, which have essential and protective functions. Laughter, which involves contraction of fifteen facial muscles, bursts of breathing, and uncontainable vocal sounds, seems to serve no apparent biological purpose. It could be called a "luxury reflex." Its only function seems to be providing relief from tension — though, when you're stressed, it ceases to be a luxury!

Add humor to the picture and it turns into multilevel teamwork. Typically when you stimulate a reflex it responds on the same physiological level, as for example when the doctor knocks your foot below the knee, provoking an automatic upward kick. Deciphering a joke requires complex mental activity (an upper-brain function), and when you get the joke it activates the primitive reflex-level contraction of the facial muscles (a lower brain function).[202] Your brain gets the joke, but your body laughs.

Humor and laughter form the nuts-and-bolts of a breathtaking, mind-blowing "laughter factory." How it does so is a mysterious phenomenon and remains a paradox unique to the human species.[203]

In addition to the top and bottom brain cooperation needed for the creation and appreciation of humor, it also calls for collaboration of right- and left-brain activity: the right brain as the intuitive one, the left brain for its linear skills (many call them the three R's: reading, writing, and 'rithmetic). A joke is a sophisticated linguistic skill, and "getting it" appears to depend on the right-hemisphere brain functions. This is borne out by the fact that stroke victims with right-sided brain damage are often unable to catch the humorous twist.[204]

As we mature, the cognitive brain overrides the lower brain's spontaneous, automatic reflexes. We acquire the ability to laugh voluntarily and also to inhibit our laughter. It's a good idea to keep the production in the laughter factory flowing while maintaining a balanced output — not overly inhibited or surrendering to raucous, explosive laughter. But it's a great investment opportunity. Laughter is contagious, so we get "more bang for our buck."

What's So Funny?

It is clear that humor is a wonderful and useful commodity and we're clamoring to upgrade our rate of output — our WPM (wit per minute). So, let's go! But watch what happens when someone makes a joke. One person "cracks up" and another merely smiles. Humor appreciation varies from person to person and place to place. Some go for witty, some for wacky. Different cultures have different aesthetic ideas about humor. It's almost as if each person has his own humor taste buds.

> An American, a Pole, a Chinaman, and an Israeli are standing on a street corner when a man comes over with a clipboard. "Excuse me," he says, "I am taking a poll. What is your opinion of the meat shortage?" The American asks: "What's a shortage?" The Pole asks: "What's meat?" The Chinaman asks: "What's an opinion?" The Israeli asks: "What's excuse me?"

There's a gender divide as well. Men and women have different tastes. Men, for example, are typically more cynical and blunter. I asked a young man with a razor-sharp humor what he saw as the differences between masculine and feminine styles. "Men could take a joke. A woman can't. She thinks it's true." You're right, sir. Blunt means to tell the honest-to-goodness (sometimes skipping the goodness) truth. So why shouldn't it be believed? Another male humor-maven offered, "Women are more likely to tell jokes that have a point or lesson in them. A man just goes for funny." Dr. John Morreall points out that "traditional men's humor is competitive, with stronger punchlines, while traditional women's humor is cooperative, and expresses support and solidarity."[205]

Humor tastes may vary and change, but laughter is a universal language.

Different personality types add to the variety: Most people are not stand-up comedians, but many can interject spontaneous jokes. *Spontaneous* or *unplanned humor* involves finding humor in everyday situations. For example, in an e-mail to some relatives, I commented that it seems they're keeping a project they were working on "under wraps" since others in the family knew nothing of it. The response came quickly from the hard-working couple: " 'Under wraps'… Wraps??? Who said wraps? We're hungry!"

Some people have been endowed with a creative, imaginative wit. They can be the subtle commentators or the "life of the party," the extrovert who makes people laugh. Note that the "fountain of humor" is not necessarily the happiest person there, but the trail of cheered-up people he leaves in his wake is a merit I envy. And you don't really need to have a stash of jokes in your memory file. Just be open to humor and it will show up from somewhere inside you.

They say that people laugh harder if a joke touches a personal chord and evokes some aspect of their own experience. Here's a joke that made me laugh harder:

> *Wife to husband in a hotel room: Nice room. And these towels are so fluffy!*
> *Husband: Yes, I can hardly close the suitcase.*

Why was my funny bone particularly tickled by this joke? It's because I have a personal memory tag on the subject. It conjures up a past image of my short-term roommates in a maternity ward, new moms who kept filling their suitcases with supplies from the hospital. They were generously trying to "educate" me as well to stock up. I experienced a measure of discomfort with that behavior, and apparently my psyche welcomed the chance to laugh the issue out of the system.

And then there are the types that are happy to watch everyone else. *Passive humor* means you're the audience, whether a solo or in row H, aisle seven, and you're enjoying watching, listening to, or reading prepared material such as stand-up comedy, written humor, or a funny scene.

Whether or not we are prolific humor producers, there's one way to live our lives: be good sports, and develop the ability to laugh things off — and to laugh at ourselves.

Humor Theories

Humor and laughter have been carefully studied and dissected. We humans have been trying to pin it down to a science, hoping to catch it neatly in a net, and perhaps even cultivate and produce it in our own little laboratories.

There are classic causes of humor and laughter that have made people laugh ever since there were people who needed to laugh.

Here are some reliable humor provokers:

The Element of Surprise

Novelty and originality is an effective laughter producer. When something happens that defies our expectations, it elicits laughs. No one laughs at normal, predictable everyday events. The surprise element, the startle factor, is a major player. Notice, we don't usually laugh the second time around.

It once happened that a girl was making a party for a group of friends in her apartment. She had found a stray chicken on a Brooklyn city street (unbelievable, but personally verified as the chicken lived on the floor below mine for several weeks). At the party she asked who wanted some delicious fresh chicken, picked up the pot cover, and there was the live chicken. You can bet the girls squawked louder than any chicken ever did.

> *Some kids were enjoying a lively ball game outside their home. Suddenly, the ball flew over the gate and knocked out their neighbor's window. These kids were not Jewish but knew their neighbor was an esteemed rabbi. They were mortified, especially as their parents had warned them not to play on the side of the house. As they huddled quietly, wondering how to handle the crisis, the rebbetzin,[206] their neighbor, walked out of her house with the ball in one hand — and in the other hand she held out a plate of cookies for the boys, who she knew would be feeling badly about the incident.*

First, we lead the person in one direction. Then, we pivot for the surprise. Though this second anecdote is not about outright humor, it stirs up an inner ripple of delight. Let's be on the alert for the unexpected turnabouts; even the non-witty ones can tease our laughs out. Life is full of these "Oh!" moments as grapes in a vineyard. These are golden opportunities to press some more pleasure out of our daily grind.

A *paraprosdokian*[207] (you can have fun just by making a game out of pronouncing this weird word) is a figure of speech in which the latter part of a sentence or phrase is surprising or unexpected; it has what we call an "O'Henry ending";[208] it elicits a surprise-chuckle.

> *Where there's a will, I want to be in it.*

> *Secret: something you tell to one person at a time.*

> *Inflation: cutting money in half without damaging the paper.*

Release from Tension

One long-standing theory is the concept of release from tension or at the passing of danger.

A woman is walking on a deserted street during twilight. She hears steps behind her. Suddenly, she hears the person quickening pace, breaking into a trot, and — gasp! — she feels a hand around her shoulder. Next to her appears... a friend. What a laugh of delight and relief that was!

There was nothing humorous in this example. Neuroscientist Ramachandran suggests that every humorous situation is based on a tension-building phase, concluding in an anticlimactic shift. When the shift reveals a "trivial consequence" outcome, instead of a more serious one, the viewer laughs. The threat of danger has passed.

A comedian intentionally creates a certain tension in his listeners, but before the climax he knocks the story off its feet in a way that runs opposite to their expectation. The tension is then worked off through physiological means, i.e., laughter. The explosive exhalations of laughter seem to "puff away" surplus tension in a kind of respiratory gymnastics. It may not be outright humor, but on a subtle level it has a similar structure: a sudden transformation of context (from danger to relief).[209]

Here are some relief anecdotes from different age perspectives:

Babies love to play peekaboo. They laugh again and again with squeals of delight. The baby is relieved and happy that the parent has reappeared. The concealment has ended, and so it repeats until the parent has had enough. Children and adults as well laugh when things appear and disappear. A jack-in-the-box pops up. Funny. (It's another form of peekaboo.) Same goes for "Boo," that playful prank that most boys love and most girls don't (typically the boo-er loves it and the boo-ee doesn't). Someone was walking and suddenly disappeared into a hole. Laughter. (Is it nice to laugh at that? Yet, countless people do when they watch comedy). He reappears. More laughter.

At a magic show, the performer asks for a twenty-dollar bill from the audience. Someone generously opens his wallet and gives one to him. The magician holds the bill in his clenched hand but it is not there anymore when he opens it. Nervous laughter. The bill reappears. Relieved laughter. The performer unfurls the bill and shows the audience that it turned into a one-dollar bill. Everyone laughs again and the poor loser laughs a little too. Once again the bill disappears, only to reappear again — as a five-dollar bill. And, finally, the bill turns back into the twenty-dollar bill which he graciously hands back to the (now dizzy) donor. They all laugh heartily as the tension is resolved and integrity is restored.

We laugh with relief when tension resolves, but we also choose to laugh to redirect tension. The startling pop of a balloon is a good example. If we begin laughing quickly we can beat the tears of the frightened or disappointed child.

We are full of relief when we experience G-d's salvation. We think He is concealed when we don't experience His overt blessings, but He was there all the time.

As a nation, we've had to experience many dangers. We're much better off today, thank G-d. Nevertheless, the Land of Israel has endured repeated aggression by hostile neighbors. Constant air alerts (recently dubbed "Code Red") giving people a paltry fifteen-second notice to scramble for a safe place has left a traumatic toll on the civilian population.

Imagine if we were to hear, especially in middle of an air alert, that the war was over and that henceforth peace would reign forever. Can we imagine the laughter that would erupt as we would celebrate the abrupt turnaround from misery to ecstasy, the transformation from beleaguered nation to eternal exhilaration!

Incongruity Theory

"Man is the only animal that laughs and weeps; for he is the only animal that is struck with the difference between what things are, and what they ought to be," said the English essayist William Hazlitt.[210] We are amused when we see children in grown-up's clothing or scuffling around with huge shoes. Imagine the notion of aging backward. Maybe then grown-ups would entertain themselves by parading around with kids clothing (it's more economical than, say, a concert). There is no dearth of wacky combinations. If you want to have some fun with youngsters here are two starters: an adult man sleeping in a crib, or eating soup with a shovel.

Incongruity has a surprise element as well. The laughter is triggered by unfamiliar and nonstandard juxtapositions of two or more concepts or images. They can be visual combinations, but the jokes we tell are painted with words. They set us thinking along one direction and the punch line or outcome throws us off by taking us in an unexpected direction. Once the incongruity of the two disparate ideas is resolved, the situation is perceived to be humorous.

A Leap Across Two Planes

Verbal incongruity requires an agile brain. Our ideas typically revolve around a single frame of reference and one plane. The creation of a joke involves the mental ability to change lanes, reverse course, and to make a sudden leap from one plane of associative context to another (i.e., two incompatible frames of reference). The listener, when he "gets it," experiences a "delightful mental jolt."

> *"Do you believe in clubs for young people?" "Only when kindness fails."*

> *An elderly Jewish man was hit by a car and was lying on the street. The paramedic bent down and asked, "Are you comfortable?" The man replied, "Thank G-d, I make a good living."*

> *David was doing well in the new country. His daughter was taken to the hospital with appendicitis and the anesthetist was discussing the surgery with the father. "No local anesthetic, please. I'm wealthy enough to afford the best. Give my daughter something imported."*

An anecdote can paint an incongruous visual image:

> *There was a chassid once who had bought into a new trend of those times. He bought the newest thing: a pair of galoshes.*

(Nobody today would think so of their rain shoes, but they must have made trendier galoshes back then!). He was quite taken with his new acquisition as he strutted around town. His Rebbe, Reb Sholom Ber, known to his followers as the Rebbe Rashab, noticed this and was not pleased. The expectation of a chassid was that he be preoccupied with spiritual advancement rather than be "into" the latest styles. The Rebbe commented, "Feet in galoshes I have seen, but a head in galoshes?"

Some people's idea of luxury is to have breakfast in bed. The night before Mother's Day, a Mom found a sign posted on the wall: "If you want breakfast in bed — sleep in the kitchen."

Some may not think this joke is funny. There goes their dream for Mother's Day.

The flexible thinking needed to make sense of the punch line takes place in the part of the brain called the prefrontal cortex. It has been noted via MRI (magnetic resonance imaging) conducted by researchers that the prefrontal cortex area was highly active in people listening to this type of humor, versus standard unfunny statements.

A Texan is visiting Israel, and stops at a house along the route to get a drink. "Come in," says the Israeli.
They begin talking. "What do you do?" asks the Texan.
"I raise a few chickens," says the Israeli.
"I'm also a farmer," says the Texan. "How much land you have?"
"Well," says the Israeli, "out front it's fifty meters, as you can see, and in the back we have close to 100 meters of property. And what about your place?"
"Well," says the Texan, "at my ranch, I have breakfast and get into the car, and I drive and drive — and I don't reach the end of the ranch until dinner time."
"Really?" replies the Israeli. "I once had a car like that."

I love this anecdote because my family had a car like that (the Israeli's, not the Texan's). If I present this anecdote to my children, the memories and chuckles will start to flow. For that alone, that car was priceless — in retrospect. A shame we couldn't find any buyers who appreciated the great long-term investment that car would turn out to be. All we got for it was its value as scrap metal. But the next time I'm driving slowly, with a flat tire or sagging muffler, I'll remember I'm keeping up with a Texan mega-rancher somewhere.

The Absurd

The absurd is funny because it mixes two qualities, sense and nonsense. The norm(al) is recast in the form of the ridiculous. Absurd is the silly end of the humor world.

Yankel and Moishe decide to pool together ten rubles and buy a large keg of vodka in the big city. They would then sell it in the shtetl at a ruble a glass. They figured they can get twenty cups out of it and a 100 percent profit.

When the normal and the abnormal meet, their encounter makes for a comic bang. Bump!

On the way home, Moishe says to Yankel, "Look here, I'm very thirsty. I have a ruble in my pocket. I'm not worse than any other customer. Sell me a glass of vodka."

"Sure," says Yankel. He fills him a glass and takes the ruble.

Soon Yankel says to Moishe, "Look Moishe, I'm also very thirsty. I'm not worse than any other customer. I also have a ruble in my pocket. Fill me a glass of vodka and here is the ruble."

A few minutes later Moishe says to Yankel, "Yankel, I'm still thirsty... I have a ruble."

Then Moishe turns to Yankel and says, "I'm still thirsty..."

By the time they came to their shtetl, the vodka is gone. Says Moshe to Yankel: "I don't understand. We didn't give any vodka away, we got a ruble for every glass... yet, the bottle is empty and we have only one ruble between us..."

Did you hear about the thieves that broke into the synagogue offices? They got away with over two-thousand dollars in pledges.

There's always some kind of crisis unfolding; you must have noticed by now that life doesn't stay boring for long. It may be something that will be forgotten by the end of the week, if not by tomorrow, but at the moment it traps us in its vice. We can find absurd angles in life's most difficult moments.

> **The more you find out about the world, the more opportunities there are to laugh at it.**[211]

> *A mom was looking for her eighteen-month-old tyke. It doesn't take much to set off panic bells when those little entrepreneurs disappear. Finally, she found her. She could have laughed with the relief itself, but (try to visualize this) — she found her little one ensconced on a shelf in her pantry.*

What if the sight is not as appealing as a little cutie on a shelf? Suppose your favorite blouse got crayon marks all over it along with the rest of the load in the dryer... or you have a flat tire. One is never in the mood for that, and it's never the right time. It would be great to have humor consultants on call, a hot-line with twenty-four-hour service coverage — after all, you never know when a crisis may hit. Right after the call for roadside help for the tire blowout, we could call the humor consultant for some Humor SOS. (Any reader who starts a company based on this idea, please let me know, and I'll feature your company in my next book for free).

I believe we're safe in claiming that Chelm tales retain their status as prizewinners for lovably absurd and at the same time benignly innocent and self-deprecating humor, while also masking the most basic truths of humanity.

> *Every morning the shammes in Chelm would go from house to house and knock on the window to wake the men up for minyan. When it snowed, the people would complain that when they came out, the shammes had ruined the pristine*

state of the snow with his footprints. The townspeople decided that they had to find a way to preserve the snow and still be woken up for minyan. The people of Chelm hit on a solution: On snowy days, four volunteers would carry the shammes around on a table when he made his morning rounds. That way, the shammes could make his wake-up calls, but he would not leave tracks in the snow.

Look out in your life and you will notice that sometimes efforts to improve things only exacerbate them. Our well-meaning governments are a great example. Do you know the definition of bureaucracy? A system that enables ten men to do the work of one. Our Chelmites needed only four! They were the wise men of Chelm after all.

Foolishness can be cleverness in disguise, just as humor cloaks problems in a disguise.

> *"Which is more important, the sun or the moon?" a citizen of Chelm asked the rabbi.*
> *"What a silly question!" snapped the wise rabbi. "Of course the moon is more important! It shines at night when we really need it. Who needs the sun to shine in the broad daylight?"*

What an apt metaphor for the dark night of the *galus*; we *do* need more inspiration where the darkness reigns.

(Additional Chelm anecdotes are offered in the next chapter.)

Caricatures, as in cartoons, mix the familiar and the absurd in the way they exaggerate a person's features, but still make the figure identifiable. A caricature can be a visual depiction, but can be well-described with artful words as well.

Those fat and skinny mirrors in museums are a high attraction for the kids, and, I'll freely admit, for us adults as well. The distortion of the person's image mixes up what is familiar and renders it absurd. The mirrors serve as an "instant caricature."

"Absurdizing" challenging or annoying elements in our life helps us deal with them. For example, we can caricature character traits.

Caricatures change the person or object's natural appearance. Some features are magnified, while others are shrunk (is that why they call therapists shrinks?).

Exaggeration is a great humor tool. When it comes to character traits, magnifying them works; then we could see the wart in all its gory glory (see our chapter on Laughter Ambassador). But when it comes to issues that threaten to engulf us, shrinking seems better suited to bring it down to size. For example…

Flat-tire humor SOS: If you hold it up to your face, you won't be able to see one thing; it will engulf your world. But move it back, further, further… Oh, look, there's more to the world than one flat tire. (Oh, did you take this literally? You didn't have to manually lift the tire. See, a sense of humor makes life easier.)

Ruined shirt SOS: Now let's tackle the shirt that came out of the dryer studded with the red marks. Or maybe a whole load-full of them. Oh, those red marks are the galaxies. G-d has invited you in to His vast cosmos. The world is great and G-d is greater. As a matter of fact, this great G-d is going to provide you with another shirt — an even better one (and this great G-d meant for us to have this challenge to grow from it). Cut a square piece off the shirt, roll two sides onto sticks (popsicle or other) and inscribe: "I'd give the shirt off my back for a glimpse into the galaxies." Hang near wash center, in kitchen, anywhere.

What would you do if you pull up at your motel and they don't find your reservation, and moreover they are full to capacity — cry or laugh? By now, we should be in the headspace to "absurdize" events or at least take them with a rueful, philosophical laugh. That's why we need to keep our funny brain switched on all the time. But just in case, keep that humor consultant's business card handy.

> I resolve to use humor strategies to enhance my life:
>
> 1. To remember that there's a completely different way of seeing a given situation.
>
> 2. To look for a punch line.

3. To remember the possibility for laughter when I encounter the incongruous — a strange uncustomary situation.

The Paradox

If the paradox is one of the souls of humor, then humor must have a Jewish soul. Almost every aspect of Judaism is wrapped around a paradox.

A paradox is a self-contradicting statement, an impossibility. It can be serious or silly. How about waterproof towels? A solar-powered torch? The New and Complete Dictionary Index? Do children still chant the ditty about "the deaf policeman who heard the noise and came and killed the two dead boys?" It reminds me of what happened at Mount Sinai when the ears saw and the eyes heard...

Only G-d, the Master of the paradox, could make the impossible happen. In the Holy of Holies, in the most hallowed area of the Holy Temple lay the Holy Ark. On some incomprehensible plane, the Ark was taking up no room at all![212]

That should explain why the Jewish People are masters of the paradox. It is inherent in our survival as well; a sheer miracle, as Mark Twain extolled: "Properly the Jew ought hardly to be heard of... [All mighty nations have] burned out, and they sit in twilight now, or have vanished. The Jew saw them all, beat them all... is exhibiting no decadence... no slowing of his energies... All things are mortal but the Jew...and [he] has done it with his hands tied behind him."

Numbers don't add up either in a Jewish budget. I noticed this years ago when I tried to figure out how my relatives in Israel were winging it on their income. Finally I gave up. The natural and supernatural merged so artfully that people just accept it as a matter of course (with heaps of gratitude of course).

The paradox is a powerful tool that drives in important values with a few disarming words.

Make the impossible possible:
An elderly woman hobbled into the doctor's office. "Doctor, I'm not doing too great. Please figure out what's bothering me."
"I'm sorry, Mrs. Neumann, sometimes even modern medicine

is powerless. I can't make you any younger, you know."
Mrs. Neumann retorted, "Doctor, who's asking you to make
me younger? All I want is that you should make me older!"

Expect the unexpected. If it's unexpected, it can't be expected! We pray for Moshiach all the time. How can we reconcile that with the well-known expression of our Sages that he will come when our thoughts are diverted from him? That would be "unexpecting the expected."

Satire

Satire reveals the absurd in the familiar, everyday aspects of life, and accentuates it by presenting it in exaggerated comic form. There are so many opportunities in the patchwork and crazy quilt of our lives.

One fellow caricatured the plethora of signs that are plastered over each other in his Orthodox neighborhood in Williamsburg, Brooklyn. They overlap like a crazy quilt, and all you could see are bits and pieces of each. One person decided to read straight across, like a long run-on sentence reading only the information that was visible without lifting any one to peer underneath. He created a hilarious brew:[213]

> *A fifteen-passenger van that will take you to Russia and Po-*
> *land for the yahrzeit [anniversary of the passing]... of the*
> *Union of Orthodox Rabbis... We check the eggs and sift the*
> *flour... on the head of a young widow who was left to bring*
> *up her young children alone after the tragic event... when she*
> *gave birth to a set of twins...*

Satire often borrows from the absurd to make its point. It does so in the following anecdote to show how economics in Communist Russia had rules of its own:

> *"The first thing you should know," one expert explained to his*
> *cronies, "is that there is only one large gold coin in the whole*
> *country, and it is constantly changing hands. This process is*
> *called 'circulation.'"*

"Wait a minute!" protested one man. "I myself once saw two gold pieces at the same time."

"Don't fall for it," responded the expert. "What you saw was an optical illusion, created by the speed of circulation!"

Satire has a serious purpose. The role of satire is to correct vices, follies, abuses, and shortcomings in society by criticizing and ridiculing them for the betterment of humanity. Although satire will be humorous, often comical, its ultimate function is not to evoke laughter. It uses wit as a weapon and tool to draw attention to both particular and wider issues in society and to influence those responsible to change their ways.

Writers of satire use fictional characters that can be easily identified as their real targets. Irony, sarcasm, exaggeration, parody, juxtaposition, comparison, analogy, and double entendres are frequently used in satirical speech and writing.

Irony

Irony describes a state of affairs or an event that seems deliberately contrary to what one expects and is often amusing as a result.

Irony: a young man tells the *shadchan* he will only marry a "skinny" girl, and rejects every prospective offer if she is not guaranteed super-skinny, and then gets engaged with a pleasingly plump young lady.

Simon sneaked off to play golf on Yom Kippur, the holiest day on the Jewish calendar, when he should have been in the synagogue. The prosecuting angels expected G-d to punish him. Instead, to their dismay, it was his best performance ever. A hole-in-one and then another one again! "What happened to the concept of Divine retribution? You call this punishment?" they challenged. "Ahh, who will he brag to?"

Irony can be a literary technique in which the writer creates a situation in order to expose its flaws and "absurdize" it. The full significance of a character's words or actions is clear to the audience or reader but unknown to the character, as in the fanciful fable "The Emperor's New

Clothes." A group of charlatan tailors got hired to make an emperor the most beautiful royal robes. They claimed their remarkable fabrics were visible only to people of high caliber. No one had the moral courage to admit a scam was going on, while they stitched away for weeks on invisible fabrics, least of all the vain, insecure emperor. Finally, as the half-clad emperor paraded in the royal procession, a guileless child called out: the emperor has no royal robes on at all! The reader knows the secret all along, and it's a secret most of us harbor as well — difficulty in admitting we are not as smart or good as we wish to appear.

"Why is it that despite so many technological advances and shortcuts we are busier than ever before?" my husband asked once when he returned from his morning *minyan*. "It used to be that everyone managed to have the time to pray undisturbed. Now they are busier than ever, constantly checking their phones for updates."

The Irony of Technology[214]

Technological progress has merely provided us with more efficient means for going backwards.

— *Aldous Huxley*

Man is a slow, sloppy, and brilliant thinker; the machine is fast, accurate and stupid.

— *William M. Kelly*

The greatest task before civilization at present is to make machines what they ought to be: the slaves, instead of the masters of men.

— *Havelock Ellis*

Lo! Men have become the tools of their tools.

— *Henry David Thoreau*

Do you realize if it weren't for Edison we'd be watching videos by candlelight?

— *Al Boliska*

> The factory of the future will have only two employees: a man and a dog. The man will be there to feed the dog. The dog will be there to keep the man from touching the equipment.
>
> — *Warren G. Bennis*

> For a list of all the ways technology has failed to improve the quality of life, please press 3.
>
> — *Alice Kahn*

Irony could also be created when we use language intended to mean the opposite, typically for humorous or emphatic effect, [215] like the "stroke of luck" that lead to Haman's downfall.

Spontaneous Humor

Blessed be the home with spontaneous humor in it. What home could survive long without it? We could each be journaling those opportunities that pop up like mushrooms after a rain.

> A wife said to her husband, who just undertook yet another two extra evening commitments, "At the rate you're going, you'll have a finger in every pie." "Mmm, then I'll have ten fingers to lick."

Our comments don't have to be sidesplitting. The brilliance of the humor doesn't matter when the purpose is to loosen the grip of the moment. Even a glimmer of pleasure goes a long way.

> I made a quick stop at the supermarket to pick up some items I needed for a party I was hosting that evening. As I was rounding the bend at the end of the aisle, maintaining a brisk pace — remember, I had a party coming up — my cart almost collided with a man pushing his cart from the opposite direction but we stopped short just in time. The man commented pleasantly, "They don't have traffic lights."

I was coasting on an inner smile of pleasure percolating from that comment for the remainder of that shopping trip. "Excuse me" and "whoops" would have served the purpose, but the humor took that interaction to the next step — pleasure.

> Tzippy and her husband Meyer set out to Manhattan from their Brooklyn home for a doctor's appointment. The trip was marked by tension about test results and pressure to be punctual, as patients more than ten minutes late were rescheduled.
>
> They managed to leave relatively on time and did not encounter too much traffic. Meyer pulled up to the doctor's building and announced with a flourish, "We have arrived at our destination. Not too bad, only five minutes late." He was surprised to hear his wife's rejoinder: "Recalculating."
>
> Tzippy, who had been preoccupied with other matters while her husband did the driving, looked up to notice that they had indeed arrived — at another doctor's office! The two offices were on opposite sides of the city. Her gallant husband- driver had confused the two.
>
> Her calm quip was to her credit. She could have harangued him about not being more on top of things. Or come down hard on herself for neglecting to confirm the address in advance. There were so many ways of responding negatively, and instead she pulled out a quick, creative adaptation of contemporary lingo — GPS talk. They set out to the correct doctor's office, with little hope of making the appointment.
>
> G-d must have rewarded her; there had been a cancellation, they were able to see the doctor, and the medical issues were resolved.

"Do you wish you had a wife like this?" I asked my husband when I shared the story with him. Gentleman that he is, he reacted like a true gentleman.

Some "Divine" News

The Divine theory: It is interesting and intriguing that G-d has been discovered in the secular worldview of humor as well. The newest theory on humor is the "Divinity Theory," meaning that humor has Divine characteristics, and strengthens the spiritual nature of humanity. All this was previously "recognized intuitively" but now it's a bona-fide "theory."[216]

The Divinity theory suggests humor has the ability to make order out of chaos by dissolving threats to the ego (such as anger and anxiety), to promote unity and connectedness through shared laughter (and connection, everyone agrees, has a spiritual quality), to uncover the raw truth of a situation, and to lift one's spirit.

In essence, as the theory goes, humor is a gift from G-d. We can't argue with the truth!

All this so aptly describes the exciting twists of fate that we call *Hashgacha pratis* — Divine Providence. When we get glimpses of these moments of personal guidance (sometimes with funny twists and turns) they do lift one's spirit.

A Ticklish Mystery

Why tickling produces laughter remains an enigma. The response to tickling is squirming and straining to withdraw the tickled "part," a defense reaction to the attacks on vulnerable areas such as the soles of the feet, armpits, stomach, and sides.

A fly that settles on the belly of a horse causes a ripple of muscle contractions across the skin —similar to the squirming of the tickled child. But the horse never laughs. A child does not always laugh, either. The child will laugh only when it perceives tickling as a *mock attack*. For the same reason, people laugh only when tickled by others, not when they tickle themselves.

Experiments at Yale University on babies under one year revealed that they laughed fifteen times more often when tickled by their mothers than by strangers; when tickled by strangers, they mostly cried.[217] The mock attack must be recognized as being only pretense, and with strangers one cannot be sure. Even with its own mother, there is an ever-so-slight feeling of uncertainty and apprehension, the expression of which will alternate with laughter in the baby's behavior. This element of tension between the tickles is relieved in the laughter accompanying the squirm. The rule of the game is "let me be just a little frightened so that I can enjoy the relief."

Thus the tickler is impersonating an aggressor but is simultaneously known not to be one. This is probably the first situation in life that makes the infant live on two planes at once.

Conclusion: Humor is "a step from the sublime to the ridiculous," but through the ridiculous we can detect and study the sublime. (That is profound!) Wait till you see what a sublime, Divine feast G-d has with humor theories such as surprise, incongruity, and irony.

-17-

What Makes Jews Laugh

J ews are widely accepted as one of the funniest group of people on Earth.[218] Sure, who had to laugh at life over the long haul more often and longer than the Jew? Many of the best stand-up comics in the U.S. are Jewish. Someone once quipped that he would consider converting to Judaism solely for the jokes.

Considering Jewish history, there doesn't seem to be much to laugh about. But if making jokes reduces stress; if expulsions, persecution and poverty forced us to sharpen our wits; if humor is another word for adaptability; if humor is a vent pipe that allows the steam to escape; if humor is a language of determination — no, the world will *not* bring us to our knees — then yes, Jews have the most reasons to laugh.

> **"Humor is an affirmation of dignity, a declaration of man's superiority to all that befalls him."[219]**

If making jokes about stress reduces stress...

Don't Jews have more stock in stress (stocks!? owning stocks create more stress. Help!) than any other nation, creed, or race? This pre-war letter is a semi-facetious reminder of the stress our (great-) grandparents endured several generations back:[220]

Zev Wolf wrote a letter to his cousin Abe who had emigrated to America, "You ask how things are going here in the Old country. The rich are still rich. The poor are still starving to death... As for the pogroms, thank G-d we could relax for the next six months. There were two recently and they never do three in a row... As for Benny, he's been out of work for a while, mainly because he's in prison. Faivel was smart. He managed to avoid trouble; he died..."

But they didn't go under. They used laughter and humor to rise above and reduce the intolerable-ness of their living conditions. They shrink-wrapped their *tzores* in *gelechter* (dismissive laughter). They turned tears to laughter when they took the threatening and menacing aspects of their lives and dismembered them by reframing them into absurd forms.

Pogroms have thankfully become relics of history but life always comes up with its new threats of various intensities. There's no escape.

Humor is despair refusing to take itself seriously.[221]

If expulsions, persecution and poverty forced us to sharpen our wits...

A man was stopped on the street in Moscow and asked, "Are you a Jew?"
"No," he answered. "I just look intelligent."

In the Middle Ages, a Jew was accused of killing a child, and faced a death sentence. At the trial, he was shown two pieces of paper. The judge told him, "I will write the word 'innocent' on one and 'guilty' on the other. You will pick one and that will be your sentence."
It was pretty apparent that both papers would have the word "guilty" written on them. The prisoner's chance of survival was zero percent.
Suddenly he had a spark of Divinely inspired wit. He picked one of the papers, put it quickly into his mouth, and swallowed it. "What did you do?" he was scolded, "How will we know what you picked?"

"Simple," said the Jew. "Whatever the other paper says, we will know that I chose the opposite." **A sharpened wit is a survival kit.**

If humor fosters adaptability...

A priest, a lawyer, and a rabbi were discussing what they would do if another Great Flood were to cover the earth. One said he would pray; the second one said he would submit to his fate; and the rabbi said, "We would learn to live underwater."

Instead of drowning in their misery, they wittily turned their misery into a celebration. They had no real weapons, but they were able to disarm and "overpower" the enemy with dry humor and satire. They twisted the threat until it became an object of amusement, something worth repeating to the *chevra* (social group) and laughing together over it. There is a fraternity in Jewish humor. We are in this together.

Some townspeople lined up to rescue a cat stuck high on a tree. They climbed up on each other's shoulders to make a human ladder. Just when the fellow on top was within reach of the cat, the fellow on the bottom who was holding up the improvised ladder stepped out to check out how things were going. "Shmerel, did you get the cat yet?" **We need each other to succeed.**

Social Laughter as Pain Remedy

A study by Professor Robin Dunbar[222] that came long after *shtetl* life was gone shows how shared social laughter raises people's pain thresholds. It causes an endorphin rush and the release of oxytocin. These are the same chemical reactions we have to touch. Endorphins are natural opiates that relax, increase trust, and promote social interaction — guaranteeing that those who practice it would continue to enjoy hanging out with their *shtetl* cronies. Whether it's physical or emotional pain, we agree that the *galus'* afflictions are a real pain-in-the-neck.

Humor is not escapist, though you'd imagine a long-suffering people would protect itself by escaping reality and indulging in the world of fantasy. It is practical and humble. The two pet topics, the hottest potatoes, were persecution and making *parnassah*. Other favorite topics were family, business, food (especially related to the holidays), anti-Semitism, health, and survival.

Humor is the instinct for taking pain playfully.[223]

We're really good at laughing at ourselves, which is a sign of strength. Insecure people don't. We have the moral courage to joke about our weaknesses, and we allow simple people to emerge as heroes.

Even the "bad guy" has merits:

> *Due a serious drought, the rabbi designated a day for fasting and prayer. All the Jews of the town assembled in the synagogue. The congregants were surprised to note the town's sinner, who was seldom seen in the shul, walk over to the shammes and ask permission to lead in the services. He explained that today he would be observing the anniversary of his father's death (yahrtzeit). The shammes flatly refused his request, but the rabbi was of a different opinion and permitted Jake to be the chazzan (leader) for the morning prayers. When the service was over, the rabbi was asked to explain the reason for his acquiescence. "The Torah tells us that sinners brought on the Great Flood," explained the rabbi. "Now, if a multitude of sinners could bring on a deluge, it occurred to me that one lone sinner might bring us at least a little shower."*

Parnassah (income) woes gave rise to this self-deprecating genre:

> *A man needs some money to cover his next mortgage payment. He goes to Jerusalem and asks for a loan. Sorry... "Strange," he mutters, "in Bnei Brak they don't give me because they know me. Here they don't want to give because they don't know me."*

*The buyer and seller are haggling over the price of some tex-
tiles. Finally the wholesaler asks in exasperation, "You and
I both know I'll have to wait a long time to get my money.
In fact I might not get paid at all. So why do you haggle like
this?"*

*"It's because I like you: the lower I can get the price, the less
you will lose when I don't pay!"*

The absurdity of the wise men of Chełm, which in real life was a
city in Poland with many learned and wise men, has become a bench-
mark for droll, deprecating Jewish humor. They took the notion of
laughing at oneself to a new level. The stories actually conceal deep
messages about truisms of life, artfully embedded. Are you surprised?
They were created by a *Yiddishe kop* (Jewish brain).

*There had been too many accidents involving people falling
down stairs. The thinkers of Chelm convened a meeting and
decided to conduct a survey of staircase-related accidents.
It showed that ninety percent of accidents on staircases involved either the top or the bottom step. A distinguished team
of Chelmites deliberated on how these accidents could be reduced. The solution was found: Remove the top and bottom
steps. It was a brilliant solution! Never again did anyone suffer an accident on a top or bottom step.*

It's as ludicrous as you could get and yet disguises equally serious messages. *Top/bottom* were survival words that preoccupied us
through most of our *galus* years. Sometimes a Jew found favor in the
eyes of the nobles, and suddenly he could find himself *teef in dr'erd* —
in the pits.

> Life, like a revolving Ferris wheel, offers many opportunities: some-
> times we're on top, sometimes... Hopefully, even when we top-ple
> over and hit rock bottom, we keep our visions fixed on the top,
> cognizant that everything comes from the one Above. It's when we
> miss that link that we're bound to think of it as an "accident."

One of my favorite Chelm images is of the man sitting in the train holding up his hands in a fixed facing position about twelve inches apart from each other. He was traveling to the big city to buy his wife shoes and he was holding onto her shoe size.

What could be more silly? Yet, you must appreciate the loyalty of this husband! Understandably, a big deal is made of Moshe Rabbeinu holding up his hands as G-d had instructed, during the war against Amalek. And here is this uncelebrated hero holding his hands up in a most laborious position for the duration of a train ride to the big city, all so he could get his wife a new pair of shoes. What dedication. How foolishly adorable! The language of love could have been born in Chelm.

Life in the *shtetl* yielded a rich repertoire of stereotypes. Some examples: klutz, *shnorer*, nudnik, schnook, *schlemiel* and *schlimazel*, shlepper, maven, shlump, yenta, and there were also plenty of knackers. As you notice just from their ring, they were created to be humor butts. Each type had their own inventive shtick, some had a *krenk* — no, not a crank — an illness, but what a rich variety of illnesses it includes. Many were humble, but so many had chutzpah! Since so many comedians were Jewish, many of these words now adorn and enrich the American language.

It wasn't only us against them. Life is more complex, of course. Ideological rifts between Chasidim and *misnagdim* (their opponents), and, later, the advent of Maskilim (the European Jewish enlightenment) opened new possibilities for internal humor, but the barb has mellowed as the controversy wilted.

Jokes today are different from the shtetl in Poland. The poverty jokes morphed into a passion for materialism and pursuit of wealth (Money! We want more and more!). Status symbols assumed high rank.

Mr. Smith had suddenly acquired great wealth. To impress his friends, relatives and neighbors, he bought two status symbols: a Lincoln Continental and a Rembrandt painting. On the day he expected them to be delivered, he called his wife from work. "I'm expecting a Lincoln Continental and a Rembrandt," he told her. "Have they been delivered yet?" "One of them came," his wife answered uncertainly, "but I don't know which."

Reaching the end of a job interview, the aspiring young graduate fresh out of Harvard is asked, "And what starting salary are you looking for?" The graduate replies, "In the region of $125,000 a year, depending on the benefits package." The interviewer inquires, "Well, what would you say to a package of five weeks vacation, fourteen paid holidays, full medical and dental, company matching retirement fund to 50 percent of salary, and a company car leased every two years, say, a red Corvette?" The graduate sits up straight and says, "Wow! Are you kidding?" The interviewer replies, "Yeah, but you started it."

Israeli politics, with enemies from without and within Israel, is a hotbed for caustic humor. Of course, there are always the cultural differences to poke fun at: Sephardi versus Ashkenazi, and the *litvak* versus the *chassid*. Jokes that were spun off the idiosyncrasies of Galicianer Jew, the Lodzer, are becoming more historic, but the punctual *yekke* versus the tardy *chassid*, the Reform Jew versus the black-hatted one, and more recently the colorful Breslov movement, abound.

The difference between an Ashkenazi and a Sephardi: The Ashkenazic Jew keeps his medicine bottle in his breast pocket; the Sephardic Jew keeps it in the lowest pocket he has. Why? Because the directions on the bottle say, "Keep in a cool dry place." A Sephardi is known to be hot and so he keeps his medicine as far from his heart as possible. An Ashkenazi does not share that concern; even his heart is cool.

Rabbi Meir Schwartz, a follower of the Sanz movement in Israel, uses humor to break down anti-Orthodox sentiment when he addresses secular audiences about Judaism:

As he prepared to address a secular audience, he was challenged on the topic of woman's rights before he ever opened his mouth. Secular Israelis were bristling after the Israeli media had highlighted alleged acts of disrespect by chassidim towards secular women, and female veneration became a hot item. How was he going to handle his predicament? Facing this skeptical, even hostile crowd, Rabbi Schwartz gained the crowd's attention by announcing importantly that a new law has just been passed. It will henceforth be illegal for ultra-Orthodox buses to drive in reverse. The audience was nonplussed. "That would put the women's section in the front of the bus!" he explained. (The so-called "Mehadrin" buses designate a separate ladies' section in the back of their buses, and this was one of the targeted butts of the secular public.) Finally he admitted he had fabricated the news about the law; it was a joke. But he had accomplished two things: He had demonstrated that gullibility may have led to people buying in to inaccurate reporting by the media, just as they had been ready to believe his announcement about the new law. And now that he made them laugh, he was able to steer the talk to where he wanted it, and proceed with his inviting spiritual messages.

Notice the speaker's strategy. He had the bus go in reverse to get out of the place the audience was stuck.

People in the U.S. seem to be less threatened by enemies from within and without, so we are free to pick on other convenient scapegoats. What a shame that we have made mothers-in-law public enemy number-one! But there's a hidden blessing in it. Now we could wish each other that mothers-in-law should be a Jew's worst enemy. (I know there are individuals out there who are thinking *With a friend like this, who needs enemies?*)

The Power of Humor in Jewish History

Humor is effective in powering our existence from our darkest moments to our climax.

American sociologist Peter Berger, in his book *Rumor of Angels*, describes "signals of transcendence," phenomena within the human situation that point to something beyond.

Among them he includes humor and hope. There is nothing in nature that explains the human capacity to find meaning even in the depths of suffering; neither is there anything in nature that explains our ability to reframe painful situations in such a way that we can laugh at them. He presents these capacities as experiential evidence of G-d's existence. They tell us there is something beyond the basic workings of our bodily systems — that there is a soul in our minds, our thoughts, and our emotions that extend to something greater than ourselves.[224] And it has the power to extricate us from the humblest and most deprived, even depraved situations to the most elevated station.

In *Man's Search for Meaning*, Victor Frankl talks about the invincibility of humor and the human spirit. From the most difficult chapter in our history, we bring tried-and-tested testimony about the role of humor:

> *To discover that there was any semblance of art in a concentration camp must be surprise enough for an outsider, but he may be even more astonished to hear that one could find a sense of humor there as well; of course, only the faint trace of one, and then only for a few seconds or minutes. Humor was another of the soul's weapons in the fight for self-preservation. It is well known that humor, more than anything else in the human make-up, can afford an aloofness and an ability to rise above any situation, even if only for a few seconds.*
> *"I practically trained a friend of mine who worked next to me on the building site to develop a sense of humor. I suggested to him that we would promise each other to invent at least one amusing story daily, about some incident that could happen one day after our liberation. He was a surgeon and had been an assistant on the staff of a large hospital." Frankl tried to elicit smiles from him by combining hope and amusement. He*

conjured [up] ludicrous scenes about life after they are liber-
ated. How the "action!" calls would be the way the medical
staff would enter the operating room while he is in the midst
of a big abdominal operation; how they would beg the hostess
to "ladle the soup from the bottom" (to get the few peas that
settled on the bottom of the thin broth), and imagine scenes
of formal dinner engagements." [225]

Another selection:

"Earlier, I mentioned art. Is there such a thing in a concen-
tration camp? It rather depends on what one chooses to call
art. A kind of cabaret was improvised from time to time. A
hut was cleared temporarily, a few wooden benches were
pushed or nailed together and a program was drawn up. In
the evening those who had fairly good positions in camp —
the Capos and the workers who did not have to leave camp on
distant marches — assembled there.

"They came to have a few laughs or perhaps to cry a little;
anyway, to forget. There were songs, poems, jokes, some with
underlying satire regarding the camp. All were meant to help
us forget, and they did help.

"The gatherings were so effective that a few ordinary prisoners
went to see the cabaret in spite of their fatigue, even though
they missed their daily portion of food by going." [226]

Let's not get stuck in the past. After all that suffering (often in subhuman conditions), we set our eyes on a future that promises supra-conditions such as were never before enjoyed. At that time we will encounter a new phenomenon: laughter as a pure, spiritual entity.

-18-

Laugh or Cry?

We have plenty to cry about, no question about that. Besides the big things, there are also the "little" daily events that are difficult to endure in the heat of a crisis.

Pearl, a coworker, described a situation in which she could have gone either way, laugh or cry. She had taken her five children, the two youngest in strollers, on an ambitious after-school shopping expedition. The weather was raw but the children were excited. Her daughter would be getting new shoes, a son was going to get the coveted keyboard model that the store said had finally come in, and another would be getting a new bike.

The shoe store was the first stop, but they left empty-handed, as the right shoes were not found (neither were the left ones), and headed to the next stop, the keyboard shop. As it turned out, the keyboard had not come in, though someone had assured her that it did. Moreover, the particular model they wanted would not be available in the foreseeable future. Empty-handed still, they headed to the last stop. This time a purchase was made. A radiant six-year old drove out on his brand new bike.

They had barely gone a block when a pedal came off. Mom

I know how to cry hard. Shouldn't I also know how to laugh hard?

decided against returning to the store and re-screwed it herself, eager to get everyone home and out of the chilling evening air. A block later the seat broke. By this time Pearl was laughing at the comedy that was unfolding. She tried to get her kids to see the lighter side as well, but one was grouchy at having his keyboard dream dashed, the other was thinking about the shoes she didn't get, and the third was walking his bike back home instead of driving it. Eventually, they did get more "laugh-y," as Pearl put it. To compound the tragic-comedy just a bit more, when she came home, the kickstand also malfunctioned, so the bike couldn't stand upright.

What would the experience have been like if not for the ability to laugh? Thank G-d for laughter.

> This is a good time to remind ourselves that, given the space of time, many issues that loom large now will be forgotten as soon as tomorrow's new headlines come in. The question of "how important will this be in five or ten years (or even in five or ten days)?" is a useful measuring stick.

Increased laughter and joy was heavily emphasized in these pages as a "way to go." Why do we talk only about laughter? Why are we ignoring the advantages of a good cry over some Psalms?

"Crying is reported to be a therapeutic wash, a balm, a salve for the soul. Laughter and tears are both responses to frustration and exhaustion. I myself prefer to laugh, since there is less cleaning up to do afterward."[227] In other words, "a hearty laugh gives one a dry cleaning, while a good cry is a wet wash."[228] No need for messy tissues when you're laughing.

> The two matriarchs Rachel and Leah each had their individual style through which they achieved *tikun* (completion of their mission) for their souls. The difference between the two modes: Leah accomplished her *tikun* through her crying, while Rachel accomplished hers with her joy.[229]

Laughter Creates Waves

What is the difference between crying and laughing? They both originate in the same front center in the brain. When a person experiences unusual events, they could both participate in the mix.

Suppression of emotion increases our susceptibility to stress-related disorders such as high blood pressure, heart disease, even cancer. The professionals recommend that whether we release the stress through crying or laughing, make sure we're using at least one of them.

Crying certainly has its place. However, often, crying weakens us whereas laughter elevates our mood. After crying, we feel depleted and tired. After laughter, our adrenaline goes up. Laughter helps us transcend our suffering; crying does not.

Another important difference between laughter and crying: Tears of sadness turn us inward; we cry and feel sorry for ourselves. Laughter focuses us outward. Laughter expands our vision and gives us a new way of seeing our situation. The "crier" sees only his world and his suffering. Perhaps that is what is meant in the Yiddish proverb: "Laughter can be heard farther than weeping."

Humor to the Rescue

An overweight woman may cry after an eating binge, for example, because she is feeling sorry for herself. "We become the central figure in our own tragedy. A little self-directed humor after an eating binge ("I don't consider myself fat; I consider myself well-insulated") may not make us physically lighter but can help us become mentally lighter. "Crying is important and should not be suppressed. But at some point in our upsets, in our pain, continued crying may not be the healthiest thing for us. We must begin to put what we cry about in perspective so that we can get on without life. Tears cannot do that. Humor can."[230]

There are many kinds of laughter that have nothing to do with the comic. Top on the list is the laughter of joy. It links in with tears of joy.[231] Crying and laughter apparently inhabit two ends of a continuum.

In the Era of the Redemption we will experience the consummate level of *simchah*. At that time, "G-d will wipe away tears from every face."[232] All the negative influences will be transformed into good and all that will be left are the tears of joy.

Here's a story in which there was a choice — to cry or laugh. Which one was more effective?

The Pail in the Jail

The two saintly brothers, Reb Zusha and Reb Elimelech, who later became mentors to many thousands of Jews, wandered for years disguised as beggars (in 18th century Poland), seeking to refine their characters and encourage their deprived brethren.

In one city, the two brothers earned the wrath of a "real" beggar who informed the local police and had them cast into prison for the night.

As they awoke in their prison cell, Reb Zusha noticed his brother weeping silently. "Why do you cry?" asked Reb Zusha. Reb Elimelech pointed to the pail situated in the corner of the room that inmates used for their personal needs. "Jewish law forbids one to pray in a room inundated with such a repulsive odor," he told his brother. "This will be the first day in my life in which I will not have the opportunity to pray."

"And why are you upset about this?" asked Reb Zusha.

"What do you mean?" responded his brother. "How can I begin my day without connecting to G-d?"

"But you are connecting to G-d," insisted Reb Zusha. "The same G-d who commanded you to pray each morning, also commanded you to abstain from prayer under such circumstances. In a location such as this, you connect to G-d by the absence of prayer."

His brother's viewpoint elated Reb Elimelech's heart. The awareness that the waste-filled pail in the corner of the room still allowed him the opportunity to enjoy an intimate (though different) type of relationship with G-d inspired him so deeply that he began to dance. The two brothers held hands and danced in celebration of their newly discovered relationship with their Father in heaven.

The non-Jewish inmates imprisoned in the same cell were so moved by the sight, that they soon joined the dancing. It did not take long before the entire room was swept away by an energy of joy.

When the prison warden heard the commotion coming from the cell, he came running, demanding an explanation.

A cellmate implicated the two Jews dancing in the center of the cell as the troublemakers.

"And what on earth got them so excited?" thundered the warden.

The prisoner pointed to the pail in the corner of the room. "It is the pail, they claim, that brought them joy."

"If that's the case, I will teach them a lesson," shouted the angry warden. He took the pail and removed it from the cell.

Reb Zusha turned to his brother and said: "And now, my brother, you can begin your prayers!" [233]

Look what we could get out of one story: Everything turns to joy if you know how to flip it right.

No matter what the situation, you can wring joy out of it.

That's what I love about the "Pail in the Jail" story — the bottom line has got to be joy. Despite... no matter what... We could laugh. And dance.

-19-
What Makes Children Laugh

Children, society's happiest citizens and foremost laughter specialists, deserve a prominent spot in a discussion of humor, laughter, and joy. We gravitate to children for good reason: they bring "carefree-dom" (can we coin a word?) and laughter to the adult stream of humanity.

At three to four months old, babies move from smiling to real laughs, thus becoming social communicators. As toddlers and preschoolers, they learn that laughter is used to establish relationships.

Learn from the experts in making sense out of nonsense and nonsense out of sense.

In a matter of a few years, they have acquired enough know-how to relish the fun of making nonsense out of sense. Once they learn language (after the peekaboo stage), children quickly learn to recognize incongruity and absurdity. The earliest jokes little kids can enjoy is based on familiar aspects of life, such as their names. Teachers can tap in to the kiddy sense of fun when they mix and match different students' first and last names at morning circle greeting time. This type of activity is sure to be met with shrieks of glee by kids age two-and-a-half to three. It fosters a sense of enjoyment as a group and promotes social bonding. Beyond creating a shared positive energy, humor serves as a motivational tool. At the four-year-old level, similar games can be used to teach early literacy skills. A much enjoyed kindergarten-level phonics activity is when the teacher begins all the foods on the lunch menu or the children's names with one targeted letter sound. They respond with hearty laughter at the odd-sounding unfamiliar words that are formed.

Little children think it's hilarious when you unite two ideas that they recognize to be nonsensical, such as parking the car in their briefcase. They laugh uproariously at silly, wacky notions such as eating with your ears or talking with your toes, and can be astonishingly creative in taking turns thinking of odd combinations. It's a sure way to wake them up and hook their short-lived attention spans when you want them to absorb the teacher's lesson for the day.

Anyone can be a successful stand-up comedian around kids. They don't need much to get giggly and roaring. And then we get to cash in on their contagious laughter.

A wacky session with generous use of absurdities works wonders in coaxing reserved or withdrawn children out of their shell. Having children take turns conjuring up incongruous or out of context examples, preferably in a small group, can often get selectively mute[234] children to speak. Take turns thinking of fun types of kugel. How would you like green-peas kugel, pretzels kugel, ice cream kugel? The key ingredients are being loose and silly, and lots of laughter.

Children, by age six to seven, dismiss nonsensical jokes as childish. They go for the pre-fabricated kind of jokes. They love to test their peers with riddles that have a prescribed punch line. It makes them feel wise and knowing to have answers that stump even their superiors.

Children have a way of getting absolutely stuck on things they want. A humorous, lighthearted approach works both at home and in school. Even when a child is bathed in scowls, tears, or worse, the resistance begins to melt inside — you can't be angry at someone who makes you laugh.

As adults, we should try to merge the best of both worlds — the experience of maturity and the spontaneity of youth. Maturing into adulthood doesn't mean we have to become stuffed shirts. We could continue to take things playfully and lightly in a way that eases intensity.

If only we could maintain the ability to take a flexible and creative approach to our conventional existence. At the least though, we should never lose sight of the joy of just being alive. Even the most senior of citizens can feel "young at heart" when they access their inner child ("*and we all fall down! Hahaha!*").

Having moved into maturity, we "de-egocentrize." We are ready to conceive of viewpoints other than our own. But even then, there's more growing to do. Keeping in mind that from G-d's point of view we are still His children, our "adulthood" is not the ultimate expansion level yet. There is another perspective beyond that; there is "something greater than our own existence and selves." We'll take you there shortly.

-20-
What Makes G-d Laugh?

What makes G-d laugh? Humor principles reign both Above and below.

G-d laughs? That's "funny!" We think we're the ones laughing at "real" jokes. Fact is, we've got a child's view (make that an infant's view) of the true, ultimate reality. What does an infant understand of the adult world?

The day will come when we will actually laugh at the same "joke" that has G-d laughing. In the meantime, thanks go to G-d for giving us some humor to bite on. My G-d, You have created a world that is so real that it fooled us into thinking it's the real thing.

Three close-ups (as close as we can get) of Divine merriment are offered here.

I. A High-Up Glimpse of High-End Humor

If humor has the ability to lift a person out of his box, let's see how high it could raise us above our limited worldview. Could it help us take a peek at the Divine way of seeing things? It requires a radical shift!

Every aspect of our world, including humor and laughter, has a corresponding root in the worlds above. Our reality below is a reflection of the realms above. *What is laughter in the worlds above?* Is there humor there? Does G-d have a "sense of humor"?

If it's going to make the Inventor of Wit and Wisdom laugh, that joke is going to have to be the ultimate, the epitome of brilliance, we would think.

For a joke big enough to serve for the Divine comedy, a whole world was created. Yes, this entire world was to become the prop for the Divine laugh-tique. Let's try to see things from the Divine point of humor:

Samba Dancers

Humor elicits laughs through the unexpected. What is the funniest, most unexpected scenario you could conjure up? A man walking on a ceiling? A pocketbook-sized car you could unfold and drive away in? (That is not as much funny as a wishful dream — and think what it would do to our parking problems. The government of the city I live in would not think it's funny either; it would go bankrupt from the loss of revenue of all those parking tickets.)

One of the most creative rearrangements of what is normal and familiar was on a city square in California.

They were strolling along, my daughter and a friend, passing time before their friend's wedding, idly aware of a Mexican fellow who was doing some simple dance warm-ups. Suddenly, quick as a blink of the eye, this "regular" man morphed into two short men dancing together in perfect synchrony, moving swiftly and deftly to the quick-paced lively music.

As I watched him dance,[235] my brain told me that the two sets of swiftly dancing feet were actually two hands and two feet, but who could tell? My eyes beheld four shoes and a lively couple dancing the samba, kicking right feet perfectly timed in opposite directions, dipping and curtsying and even twirling each other 'round.

Though I don't laugh easily at shtick, this *shpiel* really tickled my funny bone. I had never seen the human body used in this creative manner. It was inventive and humorous. (Watching the video footage a second time, we observed that the performer had two hats and jackets and two extra shoes pre-attached to his outfit.)

My vote for first prize for the novel and unpredictable goes to that stunt performer on a California street.

Actually, the most fantastic and astonishing phenomenon, the greatest joke of all times, happens daily in the life of a Torah-committed Jew, and we're not even paying attention.

What is the greatest "joke" of all? What is the most surprising and unexpected phenomenon in the world? [236]We are! Any person doing a mitzvah. We're so caught up in the daily tug of war, we don't see the impact of our actions. Here's what He sees, and why He finds it amusing:

On a simple level, He sees people doing (we hope) good things. But it's not simple to do those things.

He outfitted us with a fully loaded animal drive and he made our natural makeup self-centered. We have to subdue our coarse, animal natures and somehow make that uncouth nature an ally in our G-dly activities. The evil inclination strives with every wily trick possible to trip us up, but we stiff-necked Jews really stick to our guns. We outwit its tactical maneuvers and give up our compelling desires, for what? For a mitzvah!

That is the stuff of a sublime, Divine punch line. This human transcendence (which means it goes beyond ordinary limits) is cosmically amusing! As we discussed in the section on humor theories, what gets the laughs out? A sweet savory surprise, incongruity, and the leap across two planes. Could you think of two planes more discrepant than the physical and spiritual, the tangible and the ethereal?

Humor Strategy Meets with Success on High

When an angel acts spiritual and holy, it is as natural and conventional as you eating your lunch sandwich. But when a human being reigns over his inclinations (and that's harder than being an angel who has no temptations), and proclaims, "with G-d I go," this is a sandwich-eat-man scenario, a delicious treat that provides the Creator and the entire cosmos the deepest of delights.

The reason a perfect G-d created an imperfect world: G-d craved pleasure and laughter.

The purpose of creation was not that holy people would predictably do holy things. It was, rather, that we should say "no" to our natural tendencies for the sake of a higher truth. This is the miracle of transformation. Our amusement at the creative transformation of a man into two short samba dancers offers a visual image, on some level, of the way G-d perceives the transformation of our brute body into a spiritual-seeking creation.

The notion that our successes over our daily struggles give G-d an opportunity to laugh should help us, when we're feeling anti-holy, to persist in the standards we pledged to keep.

G-d doesn't laugh as a release of tension, because He doesn't experience tension. He doesn't laugh at the typical novelty, because He is omniscient; nothing is novel or unexpected for Him. G-d is not ticklish, but He is tickled when His inner plan for Creation is realized. He laughs at the delight of transformation and success — ours. That is spiritual merriment.

I hear the startled titters of startling but delighted surprise of bystanders on the video of the Mexican samba dancer replaying in my mind.[237] It makes a good starting point to imagine G-d's delighted discovery (are they sounds or soundless, I wonder?) of our transformational triumphs, maybe exclaiming to His hosts of angels: Whoa! Did you see what so-and-so just did for me! That was simply novel — and absolutely delightful!

The greatest source of amusement on High is that the human being can, and will, be holy. That is why the first child to be born a Jew was named Yitzchak, meaning "he will laugh," in the future.

We may not actually hear the laughter, just as we can't see G-d. But, take the experts' word for it: G-d loves the humorous twist. We are fulfilling the purpose of creation. Thanks, sir. Thank you, ma'am.

In a joke, we only laugh at the conclusion, after we get the punch line. So it will be with us. The brilliance of G-d's humor is still beyond us. Our minds cannot fathom what we cannot conceive.

"Only at the end of history, when Moshiach comes, will be able to 'get it' " — get the whole picture, and truly start laughing."

Two souls floated past each other in heaven. One was on the way "down" to be born and the other was on its way "up" after finishing its earthly stay. The descending one called out. "Tell me, are you just coming from the world?" "Yes!" the rising one answered. "Could you tell me, what is it like? What is there for a soul to do down there? It was so ideal up in Heaven." "Down there, there are Commandments!" the ascending soul calls back. "Ahhh, yes!" The descending soul said excitedly. "Up in heaven they talk about them. Even the angels go wild when someone does one. But I've never seen one. What are they?" "What are they!?" exclaimed the rising one as the distance between them widened. "They are the inner will of G-d Almighty. And you can get them just by giving the right person a few pieces of paper called 'money.'" "Wow! Just a few pieces of paper?" yelled the descending soul as the distance between them widened. "That's great! I can't wait!" "Oh, but just one thing I didn't tell you," yelled the ascending soul who in a few seconds would be too far away to be heard, "Until you get those pieces of paper... your soul can pass out!"

Which Name of G-d Causes Laughter?

A soul comes down into the world. It's got a mission to do, in partnership with the body. It's a risky venture. The mission: to find G-d.

G-d is here in this world, but He created this world with His name Elokim, a name associated with a contraction of the Divine lights.[238] (It is numerically equal to *hateva*[239] — the nature; G-dliness is concealed behind a façade we know as nature.)

About the mission... Everything in this world is designed to distract us and present obstacles to success. The food on our plate wants us to enjoy it as an epicurean delight, our job wants to drown us with its workload. We have to remain insistently conscious of the real reason we're here.

We're here to cause G-d delight. When a person subordinates his body to his soul, guess what happens? We evoke Divine laughter. "[The name] Elokim has made laughter for me —*tzechok asah lee Elokim*."

The Divine laughter and delight comes about through our toil in this world, every time our good inclination is victorious in a struggle.

So it is worth the risk... don't you agree? When we humble and subdue our natural instincts for Divine purposes, we bring about a tremendous ascent for the soul and cause the greatest delight on High.

This explains the puzzling choice of the name Elokim, a name associated with constriction, in a verse that references to laughter.

Apparently, Elokim is the chief contributor to the laughter.

It's only because G-d was able to conceal and screen His greatness that Creation could take place. If the name Elokim would not have concealed Divinity, the Divine pleasure and laughter could not have ensued. "Laughter has been made [possible] for me — thanks to Elokim."

This verse reminds us that Divine laughter will spring forth specifically through us.[240]

Next time we're asking G-d to make us happy, let's remember we have a chance to do the same for Him.

II. Novelty Woos the King

Let's think back on a stage in history that none of us has experienced. The Holy Temple is in full glory. We offer sacrifices on the altar daily, on special days, and whenever one desires.

G-d loves our sacrifices. It feels good to do something that offers Him pleasure, but we wonder: What makes the sacrifices a potent source of Divine pleasure? It's hard for us to understand the Divine workings, but this analogy will be helpful to illustrate the issue:

A simple tenant farmer wanted to acquire his own small piece of land. It would help him to provide for his family's needs. He could keep a cow to supply them with milk and grow vegetables on it, and even sell some. The only way he could get a piece of land was by way of petition to the king.

But how could he, a simple commoner, capture the king's attention? What could he do to win the king's good graces? He was a simple person, and the chance of his request being considered was extremely remote. He could not charm the king with captivating eloquence, or eye-catching petitions. He decided that the only way he could catch the king's attention was by presenting the king with something novel. With great difficulty, he managed to acquire a parrot and had it sent in to the king's chamber. The king saw a bird in his palatial chambers and wondered what this bird was doing there. Suddenly, the parrot called out the four words it had been trained to say, "Give it to him! Give it to him!"

The novelty and unexpectedness of the parrot's performance got the king really tickled, and he began to laugh. He found the whole scheme so thoroughly amusing that he exclaimed, still heaving with laughter, "Give it to him, give him what he wants."

Novelty arouses amusement and mirth, and mirth opens channels.[241]

A Word from Our Parrots...

Faivel at last could see a way of making a fortune. He had trained his parrot, after months of hard work, to tell jokes. At last he felt ready to cash in on all his hard work, and took the parrot down to his club. "This is my incredible joke-telling parrot," boasted Faivel. "Go on," jeered the club regulars. "We'll give you ten to one that your parrot can't tell us a joke." "All right," replied Faivel. "I accept your bet." But try as he could, Faivel was unable to make the parrot talk — let alone tell jokes. On the way home Faivel shook the bird and shouted: "Why did you keep quiet? You made me lose a ten to one bet!" "Don't worry!" squawked the parrot. "Tomorrow you'll be able to get fifty to one."

(A reminder that often... no, usually... no, always when you think your mazel is down, it's really on the way up, so keep the joy flowing.)

The pleasure and delight[242] we bring to G-d through the sacrifices on the altar of the Holy Temple is like the parrot in the king's chambers. The juxtaposition of our humanness (which naturally gravitates to earthly existence) with the concept of sacrificing of oneself (represented by the animal sacrifice) is a novel source of delight and amusement on High. He is so tickled by its exciting novelty that he happily accedes to our requests and accepts the prayers of our hearts.[243]

Sacrifices are G-d's funny business.

III. Divine Irony

In the second chapter of Tehillim, we come across an interesting phrase that tells us that G-d laughs, too (as it were). "He Who sits in heaven, laughs."[244] Divine laughter is directed at the fact that evil generates its own annihilation. It is a laughter tinged with irony. In irony, the opposite of what we expected transpires.

The stories of how evil falls in the hands of the righteous are mystically based events tinged with ironic, humorous twists of fate. Did we ever pay attention to the humor of the plot in Egypt — of Pharaoh raising his rival in his own palace?

Irony was described in an earlier chapter as a literary technique in which the full significance of a character's actions is clear to the audience or reader although unknown to the character. The Megillah may be written on parchment, but is filled with irony.

Do we chuckle at the creative twists and ironic turn of events as we listen to the Purim story? Three times Haman "fell into the very hole he had dug for his enemy."

First was when the roles were reversed when Haman got the underdog role while Mordechai got to wear the king's cape and ride on the king's steed.

An extra monkey wrench is thrown into the convoluted plot when Haman's daughter aims garbage at the family enemy, unaware that she is targeting her own father.

And finally, Haman is hanged on the gallows he had himself prepared. (Notice that he had prepared a gallows that was fifty cubits high. It was unnecessarily tall. How did Haman know that his archrival would need all that height so that he, as well as his ten sons, would fit? He had made the gallows the perfect height for a perfect fit for himself and his ten dear sons.)

Besides the nationally established festivals of rejoicing, Chanukah and Purim, there are cities that established their own annual Purim celebration for their city's deliverance from grave danger. Our nation has a lion's share of celebrations of happy, if often ironic outcomes to heart-stopping threats to our survival.

It's nice to know that G-d is laughing with us. When G-d laughs, we gain.

Section VI

Joy Beyond (The Mind)

-21-

The Control Paradox

I Regained Control with a Good Laugh

I was in the airport, on the way to a family simchah (an up-sheren, boy's ceremonious hair-cutting ceremony), and as often happens, there was no time to waste if I wanted to catch my flight. I had two pounds of fragile shemurah matzah in one bag, two pans of homemade cheesecake to be used for the dessert table in another bag, and my personal paraphernalia in the carry-on.

At the first security checkpoint, my progress was barred until I would compress the amount of my carry-on packages. What made this complicated was that the matzos could not be combined with the chometz'dig (non-Passover) items. I hastily reorganized my belongings to accommodate, but was now overloaded with unbalanced luggage that was too unwieldy to maneuver quickly. The clock was ticking on its own inexorable route around its circuit. As I tried to walk/run with my lopsided load that kept tipping over, I realized that my chance of making the flight was in jeopardy.

What does one do in a situation like this? I felt so out of control that I began to laugh. I laughed because I thought what a funny sight I must be.

I laughed, as well, because I subconsciously understood I needed to find strength that I didn't have. By laughing, I was submitting to G-d, as if I was telling him: "You know how ridiculous and impossible my plight is at this moment. I am laughing because I am acknowledging that this (as everything else) is out of my hands. I am laughing because I know that You, dear G-d, do have the means of helping me overcome this obstacle."

> Laughing to G-d is a form of prayer. Without G-d, I might as well cry. With G-d, I laugh. Whenever you're stuck, use laughter to get you out. Don't let life pull you down.

Things are funny if we allow them to be. When we put G-d in charge (He *is* in charge — when we acknowledge it), life could be a steady uninterrupted stream of laughter.

Sometimes, the mind needs help to close down and sometimes it needs help to expand. Laughter and humor have that paradoxical ability to both hold on and to let go. We employ L&H Inc. when we feel completely helpless, and "the carpet was swept out from under our feet." It helps us regain control.

If laughter is our prayer, it may be that humor is His answer. Or is it the reverse? You get the idea: Enjoy thy humor and laughter and keep it holy.

And we employ L&H when we're locked into our control mode. Then we need to move in the opposite direction — to relinquish control. Three "gotta-be's" that try to control us are: "It's gotta-be Now!" "It's gotta-be This Way!" "It's gotta-be My Way!" It's good to keep humor tools handy so that we can get a grip on them before they get us.

There isn't only one right way.

A rabbi was facing two disagreeing parties. Shimon and Levi each passionately stated his case, striving to be as convincing as possible. The rabbi heard each claim patiently, and then he turned to Shimon and said, "You are right. Then he turned to Levi and said, "And you are right." "But how could both be right?" wondered the disappointed businessman who had come in with them. "You are also right."

I must make a note of this... It doesn't have-to-be only *one* way... and I don't have to be right every time.
Good news: just because he's right doesn't make me wrong anymore. I'm glad I smartened up. I could probably have heated my house all winter with the energy I invested in being right (though it does take the fun out of being right if the other guy is right too).

A charity collector heard Moshiach is coming. He had one request: Since he had bad knees and going up and down to so many homes was hard on him, he asked only that his route be improved, that all homes would be upgraded to have better access. No more steps. That one change would bring him eternal bliss.

This poor fellow was so stuck in his "box" that he couldn't conceive that a truly different reality was going to unfold. We probably don't realize how often we impersonate that poor fellow. Like the tykes who choose the pennies over the dollar bills, we often get wrapped up in our small-sized goals when greatness is waiting around the bend.

I must make a note of this: I must be on alert to allow growth and expansion into my life.
I must try to think big...

Mind-blowing

Rebecca was a kindergarten teacher. One day, during her art lesson, as she was walking around the class observing the children while they were drawing, she stopped at little Leah's desk. Leah was working very diligently at her work. Rebecca asked, "What are you drawing, Leah?" Leah replied, "I'm drawing G-d, teacher." Rebecca paused and then said, "But no one knows what G-d looks like, Leah." Without looking up from her work, Leah replied, "They will in a minute."

In the world of Beyond, we shrink back to a childlike status. No matter how smart, educated, successful we are, near the Infinite Wisdom we are all limited beings. The wisest, most creative of men with the greatest of credentials and the simpleton are all equally distant from the infinite knowledge of G-d.

How much bigger are we going to make the Atlantic Ocean if we add one cup of water? One hundred gallons? Any contribution is laughably inconsequential. All the more so with the Divine perspective; no amount of human knowledge adds anything whatsoever to Him.

We understand existence from our egocentric point of view. Even when we think we're seeing another perspective, somehow we graft our own life ideas onto it. We can't think past our reality; how, then, can we imagine another reality?

The mind erects barriers. Good sense, reason, logic. Can we break the barriers erected by our minds? Can we rise above the realities around us and place our trust in a higher power? Can we let go of the security posts and make a leap into the unknown area governed by G-d?

> Make a note of this: Joy breaks barriers.

Holy Foolishness (formally known as Holy Folly)

We all know "Stop being so silly!" — either as parents or when we ourselves were children.

"Start being silly" sounds ludicrous.

Children are enchanting, but they are also egocentric and emotional — a volatile combination — which is why we are asking for trouble when we take them into a candy store or a toy store. As they mature, "they" become "we." We learn to inhibit our emotions, we become rational, reasonable beings. Nevertheless, we remain imperfect. Unfortunately, we sometimes do foolish things. Our sages tell us that a "spirit of folly" (a *ruach shtus*) causes man to sin.[245]

A person only sins as an act of sheer stupidity. What person in his right mind would want to create a rift between himself and his Creator?[246]

When we want to overcome a weakness, advises the Rambam, we go to the opposite extreme. For example, a stingy man can be extra charitable. When a person sins, it is a loss of self-control (impulsivity won out). We counteract that by shedding our controlled demeanor for a holy purpose. "Holy folly" (*shtus d'kedusha*) means letting go in a holy way, with a holy abandon. We suffered a lapse because we didn't "use our brain," and so we go from under-use of brain to supra-rational. Rav Shmuel bar Yitzchak (and other sages as well) would dance intensely at weddings, his body, hands and feet flying in all directions. His lack of inhibition disturbed his colleagues. It is a mitzvah to make a *chassan* and *kallah* happy, but a modicum of decorum should be retained! They reproved him, "You are an embarrassment to Torah scholars!"[247] G-d approved of his unabashed antics. At his funeral, a pillar of fire in the shape of a myrtle branch separated his bier from the people who were escorting him. It was a clear vindication of his "foolish" behavior.[248]

King David provides another uninhibited dancing model. Measured steps and majestic dancing could not contain his ecstasy at the Ark being brought up to Jerusalem. He flew, whirled and leaped, making him look like a "mindless fool" in his wife's words. But G-d was pleased with his holy folly.

Go ahead and make a fool out of yourself! Tap into the uninhibited, silly behaviors you had dismissed with your childhood. Don't be afraid to let your joy for someone else's celebration hang out. And that "someone else" can be G-d: we rejoice with G-d's joy on Simchas Torah and any time we do a mitzvah as well.

A prophet, when he received prophecy, was called "crazy" because he was in a state that was divested of himself and of his self-contained state, so that G-d's light could shine in him. Have we uncovered a crazy-with-joy prophet phenomenon? I'm crazy over my favorite ice-cream flavor, but are we starting a new line of flavors to go "nutty" over? The flavor of faith, the flavor of holy folly... Jesters were seen as fools. They were therefore able to tell the truth to the most powerful rulers and dictators, without censure.

If you have difficulty getting out of your box, remove your "self" from the equation. Your egocentricity is getting in the way — you're grown up now and can disengage your un-inhibition from your egocentricity.

We could serve our egocentric smallness or attach to His infinite greatness.

The low and high route of folly: The high route of folly is the route for the person who has tasted and tested the low route of folly. His soul spurs him to the opposite extreme in a rebound effect. One who struggled in the darkness seeks out the light with an impetuous passion. There's a wonderful joy in the finding.

David, the great Jewish monarch, danced with the passion of a *baal teshuvah*. His history fit the bill of the *baal teshuvah*. His unseemly blunder with Batsheva (though he did not commit a sin of adultery; see *Shabbos* 56a) led to a lifelong state of atonement. On top of that, David was descended from Yehudah, who spent years doing *teshuvah* for a series of messes. His ancestress Leah was represented as the *baal teshuvah* in contradistinction from Rachel.

Shaul descended from Rachel (through Binyamin). She represents the service of the *tzadik*. Michal's father Shaul would never compromise his regal demeanor. He represented the measured path of the *tzadik*.

The puzzle pieces fit together perfectly. At the time of the Redemption (as we will discuss in more detail in "Origins of Laughter"), the *tzadikim* too will merit the quality of the *baalei teshuvah* who achieve the deepest connection with **Genius may have its limitations, but stupidity (it surely refers to holy foolishness) is not thus handicapped."[249]** G-d, all the way in to His inner Infinite essence, a place not expressed by any of His traits, and not available any other way except through the path of mindless attachment.

The Flavors of Folly

The power of *mesiras nefesh* (self-sacrifice) is an expression of folly.[250] Rationally, it doesn't make sense for a person to be ready to give up his life, or his livelihood — but Jews "live" that way.

> *A professional comedian described how difficult it was when he initially began to keep Shabbos. His most important and highest paying performances were on the weekends. "How will I survive?" he worried. But he took the leap, and the good news is that he is thriving, financially and professionally.*

There is another way to practice holy folly. We call it a "leap of faith." Leave your mind, and submit to the Infinite powers of G-d ("let go and let G-d").

That's folly! How can I do that? What person of sound mind would rely on a salvation from a source they cannot foresee? The heart cramps with fright. But we transcend our own logic and qualms and place our trust in G-d. That's how we followed Moshe into the desert, and live each day with faith and trust in His salvation.

We sometimes have more success when we play the part of the fool. When it comes to understanding G-d, every person is like a fool. As a matter of fact, if we'll accept that G-d knows what He's doing, the business of joy would be booming.

"As a young all-knowing teenage fool, I was certain that I was a mega-genius... And like all the mega geniuses who have come before me I have slowly learned to enjoy my ignorance. It's such a pleasure to relinquish the facade of 'I know.' It's so much lighter to live in the mystery of life, the luxury of not knowing." [251]

G-d has placed among us also His agents — the righteous people of each generation who guide us. They may tell us to do something that goes against all rhyme and reason, but when we make the leap of faith, we are blessed with success.

We can get stuck in our limited capabilities, or have faith in His unlimited capacities.

One Shabbos day, a couple returning home from shul opened their door and discovered an awful sight. The town drunkard lay dead in the entrance room. A chunk of challah next to him provided a clue. Apparently he had helped himself to the delicious challah after he broke in and choked. The terror-stricken couple realized that this could lead to false libels and pogroms. In a panic, he set off to his Rebbe, Reb Shlomke.[252] The Rebbe realized the gravity of the situation and told him to take a spoonful of his cholent, bring it to his home and put it into the dead drunkard's mouth. Feed a dead man? What folly! But he had complete trust in his Rebbe. He came home and tried to get the cholent in, but dead men don't open their mouths and don't swallow. Desperately, the man urged, "Reb Shlomke said I should feed you this cholent." The lifeless corpse opened his mouth and allowed the man to stuff in the spoonful of cholent. Immediately, the dead man rose and walked out of the house. The Jew followed behind him as the zombie-like figure walked across the town. When he reached his own residence he collapsed, lifeless once again.

Infinite G-dliness is beyond the reach of our intellect, beyond our imagination, completely incomprehensible.

Step Aside

I could use G-d's hugs. I would like to tap into the Infinite aspects that transcend those lofty levels. Where do I find the code? There isn't any. No route will provide access to that lofty, Infinite level, because it is above the ordered levels of G-dliness that manifest through Creation. There is nothing to "do" except to move our (rational) selves out of the way. This level of G-d is available for us at all times, as long as we don't block it.

To draw sunlight into a house, no magnetic devices, vacuum suction, new technologies or old gimmicks are needed. We simply open the shutters and voila — the sun shines in. If we stand in the window, we may interfere with the sunlight that wants to stream in and illuminate everything in its path.[253]

Let's get ourselves out of the way. Our heads and hearts, with their desires, rationales and reasons… don't let them block the light that gives us extra support to carry through with our mission in a time of extra and redoubled darkness.

We could use every bit of light. We will use it for the joy.

-22-

The Origins of Laughter

Whether we are humorous or serious, we're all going to be laughing in the future when "our mouths will fill with laughter."[254] But where did laughter start?

Laughter is no modern invention. At first glance, when we read through the Torah, it all seems so serious. But when we look closer, we find laughter in the most climatic moments.

For example, perched on the brink of destruction, the Torah identifies a potential comedian: When Lot urged his sons-in-law to leave the city of Sodom before it is destroyed, they laughed at him. The notion of destruction was so utterly ridiculous and implausible in their nice and smooth world that they amusingly viewed his entreaty as a "spiel." The Torah reports that "he seemed like a comedian in the eyes of his sons-in-law."[255]

Now that we've spotted a sense of humor lurking, we know that laughter can't be far away.

The Torah's first record of laughter predates that by a day. After many childless years, our childless Patriarch Abraham and Matriarch Sarah were informed, at the age of ninety-nine and eighty-nine respectively, that the unbelievable was about to happen: they would finally be blessed with a child!

Let's check out the couple's reaction. Both laughed in response to the amazing news. Laughter in the Torah is meant to be taken quite literally — actual physical laughter.[256]

However, it seems the word used for laughter has a different connotation in each situation. "Abraham fell upon his face and laughed."[257] Targum Onkelos offers the Aramaic translation for the word "*va'yitzchak*" as "he rejoiced."

When the Torah reports Sarah's laughter,[258] Onkelos used a word that implies that "she scoffed." She thought it was out-and-out ridiculous. It's not surprising, considering her news source was one of three Arab passersby invited in by her hospitable husband. Her response was met with a measure of disapproval from on High. G-d asked Abraham: "Why did Sarah laugh (in other words, express disbelief)?"

In Defense of Sarah

Most commentaries agree that she did not sin in the literal sense, though her laughter could be construed as such. Some explanations: outwardly it appeared to be a sin, and thus it was termed a *cheit*, which means a failure to respond in the best possible manner (rather than an outright *aveira*, sin). She took the lesser of two *good* choices, rather than the wrong choice. An alternate explanation: her skepticism may have been justified (at eighty-nine years old!); nevertheless she could have taken the advice proposed by the Sages: "A blessing of a simple person (in this case, the traveler) should not be taken lightly." [259]

At any rate, we see in these first instances of laughter that it can go either way. It can meet with approbation from on High, or may be tinged with negativity. Abraham's laughter was seen in completely positive terms, while Sarah's laughter is seen as tinged with skepticism. But she more than made up for the halfhearted laughter, as we will see.

When the baby was born, Sarah sang a song of thanksgiving: "G-d has made laughter for me. Whoever hears will *laugh for me*."[260] In other words, "they will rejoice for me." According to the Midrashic interpretation, their laughter was over their own good fortune. Many infertile and sick people were remembered and cured on that day, and there was much cheerfulness (*schok*, a word closely related to *tzchok*) in the world.[261] Not only did Abraham and Sarah laugh when they heard the good news, they also named their son Yitzchak — "he will laugh," to commemorate and celebrate the laughter. In truth, it was G-d who instructed the first Jewish-born baby be named as an ongoing reminder to laugh.[262]

Wouldn't it be nice if we would remember G-d's instruction when we encounter a Yitzchak? "Yitzchak (oh, right... I need to laugh! Ha! Ha! Ha! Life is amazing), can you get over here now! Your supper's getting cold..."

Yitzchak has a singular connection to our joy-filled future. "Yitzchak is the one who will carry the lineage of the Jewish nation."[263]

Chava, Noach, and Sarah

Our matriarchs empowered us and enriched our future destinies in many ways.

The *Zohar* tells of three biblical giants who attempted to achieve authentic *simchah*: Chava, Noach, and Sarah.[264] Chava was ensnared by the serpent, Noach became drunk, and Sarah, the third one to try *simchah*, succeeded. She was instrumental in a major breakthrough with positive long-range effects — the achievement of genuine, ego-less *simchah*.

Why did she succeed where the others failed?

Chava started life with her husband, Adam, in a prime real-estate location. The world looked pretty good from their perspective, but they knew they were expected to further upgrade it. Otherwise, why would G-d have gone through the trouble of creating a world with such myriad detail and finish his creative process by creating Man?

Chava set out to introduce a more exalted state of perfection in the world.[265] She knew that the ultimate mode of serving G-d is with joy; it has the power to bring the revelation of G-dliness down into this world. Wine holds the power of joy, so she plucked a bunch of grapes and squeezed it to make wine for her husband.

Unfortunately, her wine failed to achieve its goal. The wine was pure, but her intent was sullied. The Torah describes how she perceived the tree: it was desirable to the palate and it was delightful to the eye. This does not portray a pure, unadulterated, and altruistic motive. Her intentions were polluted by her anticipation of personal pleasure and gain. Her perception was sensorial. Genuine *simchah* has to be pure. Strike one.

The next attempt to harness genuine joy and bring the world to its state of perfection was made by Noach. After he survived the Flood, he planted a vineyard. By drinking its wine, he planned to correct the sin incurred with the Eitz Ha'daas (Tree of Knowledge). He would taste it, he would perceive it through his senses, but he would sublimate it (make it noble and pure) and thus he would release pure joy into the universe. Instead of his plan leading to the coveted goal — the experience of *simchah* with complete self-nullification (*bitul*) — it led to drunkenness. Although a drunken man is oblivious, he is not the model of *bitul*. Unfortunately, the oblivion of the drunken person is not an outgrowth of humility; it's just a mixed-up, drunken mind. Strike two.

Finally, Sarah had her turn at rectifying the fault that Chava had set in motion. Fortunately, she succeeded in achieving the desired *tikun*: *simchah* that arises from (and coexists with) a state of complete *bitul*. Sara was able to do this because her soul derives from the sphere of *malchus*, royalty (the translation of Sarah is "princess"). Royalty, which we may find difficult to believe, is related to humility. The faculty of *malchus*,[266] as Kabbalah explains, is able to lower itself — its royal nature will ensure it rises again. And though it does so with a sense of distinction, it remains nevertheless the essence of *bitul*. A king, though he may be expanded and joyful, does so without an inflated ego. Sarah and her husband Abraham descended into Egypt, but they prevailed and came out of Egypt spiritually elevated and laden with riches. It was Sarah that effected it and Abraham was the beneficiary. Sarah achieved genuine, pure, *simchah*. Home run!

Happiness that stems from personal gratification is tainted. It leads to strife and separation. The type of joy Sarah achieved and bequeathed does not mislead or have negative repercussions. It empowers us in every generation to serve G-d with real joy, but with a sense of humility before Him and in our daily interactions with other people. Joy has strength, hence the ability to break barriers above and below. The right kind of joy strengthens our service to G-d. Finally, it leads to the ultimate ascent, to the fullness of laughter and ultimate joy, the laugh-out-loud (mouths "filled" with laughter) of *geulah*.

Thanks to our matriarch Sarah, we have a pure and genuine brand of joy at our disposal. It seems Sarah was our first joy-genius (that's what I call people who have a knack for joy, no matter what happens to them).

Her success in achieving *simchah* led justifiably to her bearing a son named for laughter.

The process that began with Sarah will lead us all the way to the Redemption.

The Joy of Anticipation

Rav Elazar Kenig of Breslov asked, "How can we achieve *simchah* in these trying times? The secret," he answered, "is that we can borrow *simchah* from the future and experience it today."[267]

He will laugh, *we* will laugh. How delectably useful anticipation can be if we only knew how to wring our joy's worth out of it!

"Anticipation can be quite a potent source of happiness," says a leading happiness researcher. "It is often the best part of the event. Anticipating future rewards can actually light up the pleasure centers in your brain as much as the actual reward will," say the proponents of positive psychology.[268]

How *do* we wring the most joy out of an event? Does the pleasure of anticipation envelop us magically when we book an airline ticket, or is it consciously increased by delving into details of our planned vacation?

It turns out there is an art to anticipation. According to a recent *New York Times* article, researchers concluded that it's better to immerse yourself. "Savoring" is an active, not passive, process.[269] Here are two savor-strategies:

1. A great spirit booster is to plan exciting events several weeks or months into the future, and pointedly mark the dates on the calendar as a motivational element in our lives.

2. Immersing ourselves in the details of our destination, its high-lights, and attractions before a trip introduces novelty and gives our routine lives a lift.

It's so much fun, after the trip, to show everyone our pictures and share its high points. Which yields more good feelings, the anticipation or the relishing of memories after the fact?

Research tells us that *anticipating the future delivers more happiness than reflecting on the past.* This finding has a profound and practical application. As wonderful and great our heritage is, it is more purposeful to look forward joyously to our glorious future than to sit and reminisce about the good old days — even the best of those.

We have a motivational date marked on our calendar that those researchers would envy. It is called the *keitz,* the end of our *galus.* We are the most forward-looking people that ever walked the Earth.

We could capitalize on this anticipatory joy, nurture it, drink in the wonderful feeling that will pervade us when we achieve the true fullness of joy and laughter. Ah, the joy-kugel... I could almost taste it.

Laugh today as if tomorrow has already happened.

No level of anticipation can top the real thing, of course, but the anticipatory mode sure makes the waiting better.

Laugh and You Will Be Blessed with a Child

The unfolding Redemption is often described as a birth process. On that note...

The childless daughter of Reb Shmuel Kamenka sought a blessing from a visiting tzadik. He told her, "A spiritual remedy for children is joy." With a creative twist, the tzadik, Reb Raphael, had deftly combined two known facts about Sarah — Sarah laughed and Sarah subsequently gave birth — to come up with a remedy (segulah). And, happily, this woman merited a child.[270]

Her father later elaborated that the tzadik had derived his answer from three places: from the Chumash (Scriptures) as it is written: "and

Sarah laughed"; from the Neviim (Prophets) as it is written, "Rejoice, you barren one"; and from the Kesuvim (Writings), as it is written, "The mother of children is joyful."

Reb Shmuel's daughter asked, "If Sarah's laughter is useful as a spiritual remedy, why did G-d find fault with her conduct?"

He explained: When a tzadik gives a promise, a remedy can be employed. However, when G-d Himself promises, there is no need for remedies.

Rochel and Leah: Who Laughs Last?

Yaakov was finally married to two sisters, Rachel and Leah. Rachel was childless, while Leah had children in quick succession. However, because Leah was the less-favored wife, though she rejoiced at her blessings, her sense of deprivation is reflected in the names she chose for her children.[271]

Her joy at the births of her first three children was anticipated and the joy was measured accordingly. The events did not break any rules or shatter convention. Her fourth child, Yehuda, exceeded her expected "mathematical share" (three sons per matriarch) of mothering the twelve tribes. His name was the first to express a positive emotion — her gratitude.[272]

The unexpected gift changed "measured" joy into "immeasurable" joy — unbridled joy and gratitude.

In any joyful event, the emotional response is "prorated" according to the triggering event. It is exciting, but measured. But, if that joyous response breaks the person's *Guinness Book of Records*, it has the power to transform the person. As a result of her system-busting, unanticipated joy, Leah transitioned to a new, superior way of serving G-d.

With the birth of Yehuda, Leah broke her personal barrier. Instead of her habitual lower genre of teshuva, a service marked by prayer with tears, she tapped into a higher level of *teshuvah* — which is accomplished through unmitigated joy.

Rachel, on the other hand, was happy all along. She represents the joyous approach of the sin-free *tzadik* who dwells in the pleasurable atmosphere of holiness.

Rachel and Leah exemplify the joy of the *tzadik* and the joy of the *baal teshuvah*, respectively. Leah's crying characterizes the *baal teshuvah's* destiny to wage an ongoing struggle with the Eisavs of the world. It seems obvious that the *tzadik* is getting the better deal, hanging around with the Jacobs of the world. But wait...

It seems like there was an error, a mismatch of genetic heredity. Leah, the tearful *baalas teshuvah*, is the mother of Moshiach ben David. Leah is the mother of the Levites, most notably Moshe and Aharon, of our most prominent prophets Shmuel, Eliyahu and Yechezkiel, as well as many more role-playing members of history. Rachel is mother to Joseph, whose kingdom was not enduring, whereas the kingdom of David would last forever.

Do we have crossed lines here? It should be the reverse! Should Moshiach not issue from a pure source of holy joy, untainted by sin?

The one who "laughs last" is the *baal teshuvah*. Through his utter repentance, he is able to transform his negative debits into positive credits. The resultant joy is more intense, since his end result was quite unexpected, and is therefore a cause for joy beyond measure.

For the *tzadikim* among our readers who are beginning to feel they're getting the raw end of the deal and worry they'll be left out of the happy ending that awaits the *baal teshuvah*, a heartening ending awaits you, too. According to the *Zohar*, Moshiach will enable the *tzadik* to experience a superior state of *teshuvah* as well. We'll all be laughing at the end. No one will be left out of the joy.

The History of the Future

G-d often takes us on unbidden, circuitous routes. Sometimes we discover a treasure as a result of a wrong turn on a high-

Even if it seems you've taken a wrong turn, you can still enjoy the scenery.

way, a plane rerouted to an unscheduled destination (not funny, but a treasure would be nice), or a special-needs child who becomes the catalyst for a parent's new and exciting direction in life. Why did Dena have to marry someone else before she met her true life partner? Even when we don't find the treasure — at least we could try to find humor spots along the way! — we know that G-d is doing it for our good.

> *Beryl, an immigrant to the United States, was fortunate to find a job as a shammes in a shul. His relief was short-lived. The board discovered he was illiterate in English and he was summarily fired. He wandered around the street market area, bought some small items, sold them, and bought some more. He actually prospered. Greatly.*
>
> *One day he sat with a bank president to take out a large business expansion loan. The deal was finalized, and Beryl signed on the designated line with a scrawled X. The officer was astounded that Beryl had never learned to sign his name. "Imagine what you would be today if you knew the English language!" "I would be a shammes."*[273]

Humor Takes the Back Door

I think of humor as a back-door approach, or the undercover world of communication.

When you can't get away with telling someone something straight out, try the back-door approach. "Say something with humor and it will be accepted where a logical frontal statement will not," advises psychologist Dr. Ed. Yisroel Susskind.[274] It may take more effort to find the right way to get the message across, but the successful results will be worth our while.

Here are some "back-door" entries:

Your wife is walking around in a huff. Didn't you know that she wanted a fur coat for her anniversary? *Shalom bayis* (domestic harmony) experts often remind women that their husbands are not mind readers. He doesn't know what's on her "wish" list if she doesn't tell him. Husbands, keep this "damage-control" anecdote handy to make your point with humor:

> *Larry was sitting in the dentist's chair complaining of a terrible toothache. "Which tooth hurts?" asked the dentist. "Are you*

a good dentist or not? I shouldn't have to tell you. You should know." The dentist extracted a tooth, but the pain wasn't gone. So the dentist pulled another. And another. Finally, on the last tooth, he "hit the nail on the head" — he nailed down the source of the pain. "Doctor, you located the source of the pain. Finally!"

We meet people all the time that know how to do things better than the other guy. They can tell a joke better, cook a roast better, explain things better, exercise better (and put together a better and longer list than I am. Oh. yes, and run the schools better.) Perhaps they are descendants of Berel:

> *Berel, an itinerant teacher in pre-war Poland, made barely enough money to keep his family from starving. But what's to stop one from thinking big? Berel was overheard telling his friend, "If I were Rothschild, I'd be richer than Rothschild." "How so?" asked his friend. "Simple — I'd do a little teaching on the side."*

If we think about the way many key events in history came about, we will agree that the back-door has seen quite a bit of traffic. It seems that the greater the magnitude of an event, the more circuitous its path.

Yaakov got his father's blessings by disguising as Eisav; Peretz, an ancestor of Moshiach, came into this world by Tamar meeting up with Yehuda in a complex set of events. The marriage of Boaz and Ruth that produced the forefather of King David was superficially fraught with questions, but halachically sanctioned when all aspects of the plot were considered. King Solomon was born from David's union with Batsheva, another shady event.

> *There was a lecture on hypnotism. Simon volunteered to become a subject. "And now, I will put this man into such a trance that he will forget his entire past."*
>
> *"Don't do that, please," shouted a man from the audience. "He owes me a fortune!"*

It seems that the major players involving the origins of the house of David, and Moshiach had to evolve in a way that shrouded their import. This was in order to evade the Satan who does everything in his power to arrest Moshiach's progress. After all, when the *galus* is over he'll be out of business!

These glimpses of how our destiny is woven into our history are interesting. And useful as well, to remind us that every *galus* story — and every Jew's life is part of that *galus* story — is bound to have a happy ending. Our unshakable faith in the ultimate triumph of goodness helps us chuckle along the way, despite...

> **"Everything is always okay in the end; if it's not, then it's not the end."**

No one perceived these epic, historic events as funny when they occurred, but they say that "comedy equals tragedy plus time." We'll laugh when it's over at last.

-23-

Times Change – It's Okay to Laugh Now More than Ever...

n the future, the Shelah[275] assures us that the faith of the people will surpass that of the generation that left Egypt. When the Jews left Egypt, the men sang *after* the miracle of the Sea of Reeds. The women, on the other hand, were prepared with tambourines because they believed with full faith even before anything happened (holy folly!).

Knowing the ending is going to be happy makes it easier to laugh more, now.

Then Moshe and the children of Israel will sing — "*az yashir Moshe.*"[276] We sing this exultant song of praise, joy, and gratitude for the miraculous splitting of the Sea of Reeds in our daily morning prayers. It is couched in the future tense: "*Then* Moshe and the children of Israel *will* sing."

It also alluded to the distant future: when we are on the threshold of Geulah, *then* Israel will sing praise in advance of the Geulah.[277]

When a person has faith and confidence in an outcome, he or she could derive cheer from the event *before* it transpires. We often do so without realizing it.

On a blustery winter day, my daughter was bumping a suit-case down our front steps. It was obvious she was headed to the airport. My neighbor, who runs a car service, noticed my daughter was wearing only a light sweater and guessed, laughingly, "She's going to Florida, isn't she? I could tell right away which of my passengers are going south. They get into my van in the middle of the winter with no coats, as if it's in middle of the summer here." They are warmed in anticipation of the warm air that will greet them when they arrive at their destination. They are living in the future before it arrived!

"The righteous, as soon as they are promised something good, praise G-d immediately, even before it is fulfilled... In the future, when the Jewish People will be foretold of the Redemption, they will rejoice and sing immediately, out of full faith that the prophecy will be fulfilled."[278]

"Then" we will laugh. But now?

Is it okay to laugh now?

The Talmud tells us that mirth and merriment should always be attached to a mitzvah. The Talmud offers an opinion that *simchah* should generally be attached to a mitzvah.[279] According to that opinion, only during the month of Adar is mirth and merriment approved without direct relation to a mitzvah. But today, the aroma of the pre-Geulah joy (the kugel!) pervades the atmosphere.

The Lubavitcher Rebbe tapped into the opportunity it presents.[280] The permission slip to practice full, unbridled joy has been given to our time, specifically as a way of ushering in the Redemption. Right now, in our darkest moments, is the time to smile to each other, to laugh, to sing, and to dance. Fill our mouths with laughter!

The Rebbe expounded the verse **az** *yimalei schok peenu* (**then** our mouths will fill with laughter") based on the numerical value of the word *az*, which adds up to eight.[281]

When we reach the eighth [generation], counting from the Baal Shem Tov (and we have already reached and passed that mark), *then* we may "fill our mouths with laughter" (barring *holelus* of course).[282] We can rejoice — and *should* rejoice — because we are so close to the Redemption. We are living in laughter-approved times![283]

With the joy of anticipation, we invite the future into the present.

Then we'll laugh like there's no yesterday. *Now* laugh as if tomorrow is here already.

What's more: The amazing quality of joy we will experience when Moshiach comes, in reward for our serving G-d with joy, will far surpass the actual "principle investment," so much so that the term "reward" will be rendered inadequate.

Be happy now for the joy we will have in the future.

Isn't it wonderful that it's okay to laugh — now more than ever. Now and forever.

Epilogue
Shabbos Is Coming

How we savor the approaching Shabbos...

Shabbos offers twenty-four hours to disengage from the intense weekday world and an opportunity to renew and engage with the Creator. And... It is also representative of a new wondrous era, an era void of conflict and suffering and full of meaning, joy, and blessing. Merely contemplating this fills us with delight.

We've lived through almost 2,000 years of pain and suffering. It was a long haul, but now it is very, very close.

> It reminds me of my family's annual trek to the mountains. At the beginning of the trip we are busy worrying if we left anything behind, dealing with the city's traffic snarls, and distracting the kids who want to know if we're almost there ten minutes into the trip. But when we're finally on our last leg we succumb to the upcoming bliss. We roll down the windows to sniff the delicious fresh air, we imagine ourselves luxuriating on grassy lawns, swimming under sunny blue skies, tossing balls across fields, and taking invigorating walks on rolling country roads flanked by cool forests.

In the earlier stages of the trip the final destination was not that significant; the journey itself was a major preoccupation. But now, leaders of our times are telling us we are so close to the Redemption that we can almost touch it.

Through the earlier stages of our *galus* years, smooth riding was punctuated by turbulent local conditions. But now that we are so close, the details and the wonders that await us loom more largely. Expect joy, joy, and more joy.

Our situation today may be more difficult, and yet it is better than in earlier times.

More difficult because we're exhausted by the long drawn-out *galus*.

Better because we are closer than ever to the joyous culmination. And we have discovered so many ways to increase in joy in these last moments.

More difficult because who has time to think? Especially just before Shabbos when things are even more hectic.

Better because on Friday afternoon we can practically "smell and taste" the upcoming delight. We can begin to luxuriate in it.

Ahhh. The smell of the house on *erev Shabbos* brings back memories of our mother's kitchen... our bubby's inimitable kugel... Breathe in deeply, and as we remember the past, let's remember the future as well. It's the best way to change the present.

Appendix:
Laugh Your Way to Health

Laughter Club Success Stories[284]

"We don't laugh because we're happy; we are happy because we laugh," said William James.

A woman who was diagnosed with a serious form of cancer was in terrible pain, and unable to sleep at night. After just a few weeks of "laughter therapy," this woman reported that she started sleeping normally at night, for the first time in months!

A woman from a rural area worked on a farm with strong pesticides that had destroyed her lungs. Eventually, she needed to be on oxygen every night. Since she joined the "laughter therapy" and learned how to breathe deeply, she's off the oxygen!

A seventy-year-old woman, post-stroke, after three months of workshops and home exercise could exclaim, "I feel born anew. I can sleep, breathe and I feel great. My doctor has even given me a clean bill of health, thanks to you!"

A fifty-year-old woman with very high blood pressure was able to throw away her numerous pills when it had stabilized.

Women in depression who were incapable of laughing, even of going through the motions, loosened up after a few sessions as observers and began enjoying — life itself. One person confided that she hadn't laughed for fifty years until she began the workshops.

Laughter clubs report many success stories in the area of *shalom bayis* (domestic harmony).

> It was a sticky **shalom bayis** situation involving a couple who had separated. After four months of listening and guidance, laughter therapy, and venting exercises, the woman was ready to pick up the phone and initiate a call to her husband. They were reunited just in time for Passover, and they are doing well.

If words are the lyrics and laughter the melody, then a relationship becomes a symphony.[285]

The Health Menu

I was sitting in a restaurant assiduously studying the menu, several pages of exotic-sounding multi-syllabic words. I finally signaled the waiter for help in deciphering what the actual foods are in plain English, tripping over the pronunciation as I read them to him. My salivary glands were duly salivating despite my poor comprehension — can vegetable soup compete with Zappa di Verdure? The mysterious meanings of the options are part of the allure of the upcoming repast (meal in plain English).

Now we are ready to have a health-terms feast as we ingest some genuine technical terminology. We are likely to forget the scientific words as soon as we turn the page, but it's nice to see the array.

Of course we could just call these conditions *stress-itis* or an *inflamed happiness-index*, but hopefully our systems will be nurtured simply by contemplating the tantalizing information that spells out wellbeing.

Laughter decreases things we want to decrease, such as:

Stress hormones, which can constrict blood vessels and suppress immune activity.

- Dopamine, a chemical released during "fight or flight" response.
- Cortisol levels, which suppress the immune system. With cortisol out of the way, we allow the immune system to do its important work and protect us from pollutants, allergens and cancer.[286]

Here is another dose of medical jargon:

The lymphatic system (cells associated with the immune system) is activated through a complex mind body–feedback mechanism. Stress-produced emotions trigger the release of cortisol and aldosterone substantially. These may decrease the T-lymphocyte cell count, thereby impairing the immune system response.

Conversely, positive thoughts and feelings increase the effectiveness of the T-cells, enabling the immune system to fight illness from the common cold to cancer. Thus, laughter and positive emotions including joy, love, trust, hope, contribute to the strength and integrity of the immune system.

Medical Benefits of Humor

It's a painkiller. A person could pick which "brand" of painkiller they prefer, humor or laughter! People who were exposed to humor before and after surgery, and before painful medical procedures, perceived less pain.

A sense of humor can add eight years to your life. Add that to honoring your parents as a longevity factor!

Your sense of humor may or may not add years to your life; but it certainly will add life to your years."[288]

Higher levels of a good antibody (called salivary immunoglobulin-A) were found in the saliva of people who watch humorous videos or experienced good entertainment. These antibodies fight infectious organisms that enter the respiratory tract.

Merely *anticipating* humor, and also after exposure to humor, lowers adrenaline levels. That's a powerful before- and after-effect.[287]

Do you wish to add years to your life and increase the quality of your days? Humor is the way. Test the humor presence in your blood:

1. Can you quickly recall a hilarious memory, or a most embarrassing moment?

2. Do you regularly like to hear or tell funny jokes and stories?

3. Do you catch yourself laughing and smiling several times a day?

4. Do you laugh at yourself easily?

Answering yes to questions 1–4 suggests you have a good sense of humor. Continue...

5. Are you oversensitive when others tease you?

6. Do you reserve your sense of humor for certain people, places, or times?

7. Have you been told that you are too serious and need to lighten up?

8. Do you sometimes use sarcasm or put-downs in place of being direct?

Answering yes to questions 5–8 could be signs of a great need to develop your sense of humor.

Notes

1. Rabbi Yisrael Abuchatzeira.
2. Redemption, the culmination of all we have been working toward since Creation; a time where there will be no more hunger, strife, or illness. We will know G-d in a way we never did before, the Holy Temple will be rebuilt, and we will have perfect joy as an independent entity.
3. "Rejoicing in Anticipation of the Ultimate Joy," by Menachem Ziegelboim, *Beis Moshiach* #872.
4. Public address, *Ki Seitzei* 5748.
5. Beam with pride and delight.
6. Mort Walker.
7. Anna Fellows Johnston.
8. Raymond Hitchcock. Responses were posted to whit: Some poor people have a rich sense of humor; you can lose money but you cannot lose a sense of humor. Posted by Adam Rifkin on pandawhale.com/post/20958.
9. Abraham Lincoln.
10. *Brachos* 31a: *Asur l'adam sheyamelah 's'chok peev b'lam hazeh.* According to the Tur, this limitation applies to the Diaspora. Some say it applies even to the eras of the Holy Temple (Rabbeinu Yona).
11. 8:15.
12. 2:2.
13. 2:2.
14. 7:4.
15. *Shabbos* 30b.
16. *Likutei Moharan*, Mahadura Beis 48, end.
17. *Toras Menachem* 5745, Vol. II, p. 1112; and ibid. 5742, Vol. III, p. 1523.
18. *Sipurei Chassidim*, Rav Zevin, Mo'adim p. 188.
19. *Mishne Torah*, Festivals 6:20.
20. The Rambam and the Rama are two major halachah codifiers.
21. *Mishneh Torah*, Da'os 1:5. See also commentaries.
22. *Avos* 3:17. http://www.torah.org/learning/pirkei-avos/chapter3-17a.html.
23. *Shulchan Aruch, Orach Chayim* 697:1.
24. Ibid. 560, end, *Magen Avraham*. The quote is from Mishlei 15:15.
25. Robert Anthony.
26. Ibid.
27. Bumperstickers.laughtertherapy.com.

28. Colette.
29. Quoted in *Time* magazine, June 2, 2014.
30. Charles Kettering.
31. Shawn Achor, *The Happiness Advantage*, p. 52.
32. A.A. Milne.
33. Steven Wright.
34. The original line in Yiddish: *"Vi kricht men fun danet arois?"* Literally, how does one crawl out of here, or, how do I get out of this mess?
35. He lived in the late 1800s. Ostropol is a town in the Ukraine.
36. *Yeshaya* 25:12.
37. Carolyn Llewellyn.
38. *Magen Avraham* 250:8, based on *Zohar*. The Shelah calls it a mitzvah as part of the honor of Shabbos; see *Shabbos* 97b.
39. One thousand years for each day of the week, culminating in the Shabbos that corresponds and mimics the serene bliss of Geulah. Each millennium can be divided to correspond to the parts of a day. We are now in the afternoon of *erev Geulah*.
40. *Zohar* 1:117a. From Gutnick Chumash on *Bereishis* 7:11.
41. Yeshaya 11:9.
42. Copies in four languages are available through 011-972-73-724-6000, or by email: 9791193@gmail.com.
43. *Pesachim* 105b.
44. A revered and beloved rabbi in Poland, famous for his ethical and halachic works, 1838-1933.
45. Pleasure.
46. Rabbi Pinchos Lipschutz, in an editorial for *Yated Ne'eman*, spring 2014. The precise date was not available, and he sent the information to me in an e-mail. Rabbi Shternbuch, a venerated rabbi in Israel, is the one who divulged this historic revelation. He notes that although the Crimean Peninsula belonged to Russia for a long time, the Vilna Gaon was referring to an act of reconquest. Rav Shternbuch is a direct descendant of the Vilna Gaon. He is renowned as one of the senior *poskim* of the generation and is the author of numerous works. Rebbetzin Aidel Miller, granddaughter of Rabbi Yaakov Herman (whose biography is featured in *All for the Boss*) told me that this "secret" was known to her family as she was growing up.
47. Thanks to Chaya Rivkah Zwolinski, my Breslov connection, for finding this for me (as well as the one on dance).
48. Tehillim 100:2.
49. *Derech Mitzvosecha* 199a; *Likutei Sichos, parshiyos*, p. 186m; *Tanya* ch. 17.
50. Post-traumatic stress disorder.
51. Taken from a talk by Rabbi Simon Jacobson at a gathering after the passing of a young mother. "We cry like no one else cries. But, we also know how to build like no one else knows how to build." His remarks were based on a letter the Lubavitcher Rebbe had written to this woman's mother when she herself was orphaned at a young age.
52. Combative.
53. As the scripture says of the Jews in Egypt, the more they were persecuted, the more they flourished and grew.
54. Mrs. Frederic J. Faulks.
55. Divrei Hayamim 16:27.
56. Leslie Caron.

57. Tali Loewenthal, *The Scroll*, Aug. 8, 2014, chabad.org.

58. Mishlei 27:19.

59. "Let Israel rejoice in his maker," Tehillim 149:2; and "May G-d rejoice in His works" Ibid. 104:31.

60. The Rambam calls the *simchah* that accompanies the performance of mitzvos "a great service." This law appears at the end of the section on Succos (*hilchos lulav*).

61. *Devarim 28:47–48.*

62. Translation and commentary by Rabbi Eliyahu Touger, from chabad.org.

63. II Shmuel 6:16 The verse uses two words *mefazez* and *mecharker*, translated as dancing and cavorting.

64. Ibid.

65. Mignon McLaughlin, *The Neurotic's Notebook* (1960).

66. Leo Tolstoy.

67. Distilled from lecture series by Rabbi Yossi Paltiel; audio recordings available at http://insidechassidus.org/fall/186-parshas-chayey-sara/1001-parsha-classes-chayey-sara.html.

68. A myrtle branch is called *shutisa*, which is related to the word *shtusa*, meaning foolish. It was customary to dance before the bride and groom with myrtle branches in hand, in order to enhance the joy of the new couple. One who dances with it looks like a fool, but the sages would dance with abandon, without regard for their dignity. (*Kesubos* 17a). The sage R. Yehudah the son of R. Ilai would do so (twirl a sprig of myrtle) as he danced before the bride. Rav Shmuel bar Rav Yitzchak "mortified" his colleagues when he "made a fool out of himself" in his frolics (ibid.).

69. At the time of resurrection, the body will be rebuilt from one tiny indestructible bone that remains of the body.

70. As we get closer to Moshiach, we have precursors to the state that will reign then, namely that the soul will derive its nurture from the body. See *Likutei Sichos* vol. 1, p. 532.

71. In the same way, the feminine dimension will dominate, which is in accordance to its original Divine source. That is the reason G-d told Abraham to listen to whatever his wife Sarah tells him. Sarah is considered the Kabbalistic equivalent of the body, whereby Abraham represents the soul.

72. Gutnick Chumash, *Bereishis* p. 140.

73. My thanks to Rabbi Alexander Seinfeld for his lucid differentiation of spiritual and material pleasures in *The Art of Amazement*, Jewish Literacy Edition (2009).

74. *Avos 2:12.*

75. The soul is striving to connect to its Creator, akin to the quivering flame of a candle that constantly strives to unite with its source of fire above.

76. Tehillim 35:10.

77. *Gadol limud hameivee l'yedei maaseh* — learning is worthy when it permeates through to our actions.

78. Paradise.

79. *Shulchan Aruch, Orach Chaim* 529:2.

80. *Pesachim* 109a.

81. *Tanya* ch. 31; *Lessons in Tanya* p. 410, Vol 1, footnote 9.

82. The extra month in the Jewish leap year.

83. Spiritual matters.

84. Our thoughts are considered "spiritual" in comparison to the two other more tangible faculties of expression — speech and action.

85. *Ma ashiv laHashem kal tagmuloyhee aloi* — the opening line of a chapter in Hallel, the collection of *Tehillim* we say on festivals and for a New Month.

86. A joy that is unconditional is not measured by what we "get," or what we think is possible.

87. Gretta Brooker Palmer.

88. Tehillim 35:10.

89. Author unknown.

90. www.tmjhope.org/is-laughter-the-best-medicine/.

91. Author unknown. Taken from an editorial in *New York Tribune*, quoted in Maud van Buren, *Quotations for Special Occasions*.

92. Crying, on the other hand, a similar motor reflex, is marked by a painfully tight throat, and produces a choking sobbing.

93. Beta-endorphins are neuropeptides involved in pain management, possessing morphine-like effects.

94. www.seniorhomes.com/p/humor-and-laughter-health-benefits-for-seniors-resources/.

95. According to a study by Professor Robin Dunbar, as seen in Jimmy Carr & Lucy Greeves, *Only Joking* (Gotham Books 2006), p. 21.

96. http://www.dailymail.co.uk/health/article-1364727/Laughter-IS-best-cure-It-promotes-healing-speeding-blood-flow.html.

97. http://lubbockonline.com/stories/021210/fea_561958397.shtml.

98. See footnote 70.

99. http://www.ncbi.nlm.nih.gov/pubmed/19450597.

100. Tehillim 126:2.

101. *Shemos Rabba* 35:1. The world was not deemed worthy for gold, and why was it then created? For the Tabernacle and for the Holy Temple.

102. George Gilbert.

103. Mishlei 17:22.

104. Devarim 4:15; also *venishmartem me'od l'nafshosaichem* — take good care of your life (ibid. 4:9), quoted in *Shulchan Aruch* 32:1. It is considered a rabbinic law.

105. Culled from points sent to me by Tzipi Dagan.

106. Facts compiled by Ball Memorial Hospital in Muncie, Indiana.

107. http://science.howstuffworks.com/life/laughter2.htm.

108. Author unknown.

109. Charles Gordy.

110. Joe Bobker, *Big Book of Jewish Wit & Wisdom* (Gefen Publishing 2011), p. 153.

111. http://science.howstuffworks.com/life/smiling-happy1.htm. In 1989, a psychologist named Robert Zajonc published one of the most significant studies on the emotional effect of producing a smile. According to one hypothesis, the facial changes involved in smiling have direct effects on certain brain activities associated with happiness.

112. http://geniusbeauty.com/woman-health/5-happiness-facts/.

113. Author unknown.

114. Quoted in *P.S. I Love You*, compiled by H. Jackson Brown, Jr.

115. http://en.wikipedia.org/wiki/Mirror_neuron.

116. Mishlei 27:19.

117. Today it is a city in Belarus. Story appeared in *Ami Living*, Oct 9, 2011.

118. Rabbi Nissan Mindel, *The Significance of Chasidic Dancing*. www.NissanMindelPublications.com.

119. *Likutei Tefillot* I:10.

120. During the intermediate days of Sukkos 5714.

121. II Shmuel 6:16. The year: 2892.

122. Oscar Wilde.

123. His widely cited book, *Laughter: a Scientific Investigation*, was selected as one of "The 25 Books to Remember from 2000" by the New York Public Library.

124. Carr & Greeves, *Only Joking*, p. 31.

125. Listen to yourself the next time you're on the phone, or meeting up with a friend or colleague. In routine one-to-one conversations, the person who is speaking laughs almost fifty percent more than the listener.

126. *Tzava'as ha'Ribash* par. 3, as seen in the *Kol Menachem Tehillim*, Schottenstein edition.

127. The ability or tendency of an organism or cell to maintain internal equilibrium by adjusting its physiological processes.

128. Thomas Carlyle.

129. Carr & Greeves, p. 272.

130. They lived in a city-state in the area of Ashkelon, Gaza, and Ashdod.

131. *Parshas Vayeira*.

132. Rabbi Heschel Greenberg, "Sealing off the two open sides of the alley," *Beis Moshiach* #947.

133. I have not seen this article, but thanks to Ruchy Gottlieb for sharing the content and some valuable insights.

134. http://www.forbes.com/sites/kareanderson/2012/08/13/15-ways-to-accomplish-more-with-the-right-kind-of-humor/.

135. Elsa Maxwell.

136. Shirley MacLaine.

137. Edgar Watson Howe.

138. Jo-Ellan Dimitrius and Wendy P.. Mazzarella, *Reading People: How to Understand People and Predict their Behavior — Anytime, Anyplace* (Ballantine Books, 1998).

139. http://www.britannica.com/EBchecked/topic/276309/humour.

140. Elie Wiesel, *Somewhere a Master: Hasidic Portraits and Legends*, (Schocken Books, 1982)

141. That may be changing: Medical clowns to facilitate healing in hospitals are being professionally certified in university courses.

142. As told to Riva Pomerantz, *Impressions* (Chofetz Chaim Heritage Foundation), Vol. 8, 1. Reprinted with permission, with minor adaptations.

143. *Pesachim* 117a. Some sources name the teacher as Rava.

144. *The Majestic Bride*, translation of the "Maamor Lecha Dodi" by Rabbi Yosef Yitzchak Schneersohn and Rabbi Menachem M. Schneerson, part of the Chassidic Heritage Series (Kehot Publication Society). I am indebted to the excellent translation of Rabbi Ari Sollish, from which I have borrowed [paraphrased] freely.

145. Rabbi Dovber Shneuri, *Toras Chaim*, chapter 12 (5c).

146. http://www.collive.com/show_news.rtx?id=26933&alias=impact-of-the-rebbes-joke.

147. *Overcoming Folly* (English translation of *Kuntres U'mayon* by Rabbi Sholom DovBer of Lubavitch),(Kehot Publication Society), p. 36.

148. My thanks to Rabbi Micheol Golomb for his clarifying commentary.

149. http://www.tag.ubc.ca/facdev/services/newsletter/89/mar89-3.html.

150. James Rhem, *Humor in the Classroom*, The National Teaching and Learning Forum, vol. 7, issue 6.

151. http://www.seniorhomes.com/p/humor-and-laughter-health-benefits-for-seniors-resources/.

152. Carr & Greeves, p. 202.

153. From the Dubno Maggid, master of the parable. The anecdote describes the Maggid's unerring ability to conjure up a parable for a scenario in the blink of an eye [at a moment's notice].

154. Several humor strategies and perspectives were sparked by the discussions in Rabbi Nilton Bonder, *Yiddishe Kop* (Shambhala, 1999). Translated from Portuguese.

155. From a talk by Rabbi Y. Y. Jacobson, "Baal Shem Tov's Manual for Education," Kislev 5774, CD.

156. *Berachos* 7a.

157. A large city in Iran, and the capital of East Azerbaijan Province.

158. The story was printed in a school newsletter. I'm told it was taken from a collection of stories called *Brilliant Gems*, currently out of print.

159. Fear expresses an absence of *bitachon* — trust in G-d. When G-d is actively present in our lives, we live with (His) joy.

160. *Mishneh Torah, Melachim*. 12:1.

161. W. H. Auden.

162. As seen in Miriam Paley, "Laughing our Way through Life," *Mishpacha* magazine, April 6, 2005, p. 52.

163. http://www.britannica.com/EBchecked/topic/332293/laughter.

164. Rabbi Yaacov Yitzchak (1745–1815), a disciple of the Maggid of Mezritch. Called "the Chozeh" due to his visionary powers.

165. Robert Morreal, video. Available at humorworks.com.

166. Presentation at Nefesh Conference, Dec 2007, titled "Using Humor to Change People's Thoughts, Feelings, and Actions." My thanks to Shira Frank for a copy of the audio recording.

167. Rabbi Benzion Twerski, Nefesh conference, Dec. 2007.

168. There is no source. I just wanted to make and prove a point: "Though shalt not be gullible." A wise person does not fool himself, does not fool others, and does not allow himself to be fooled.

169. http://www.webmd.com/balance/features/give-your-body-boost-with-laughter.

170. The great whale that will be served at the celebratory feast at the time of the Geulah.

171. *Taanis* 22a.

172. "The World to Come" sometimes refers to Gan Eden, and sometimes refers to the period following the Resurrection.

173. If you would like arrange a program in your community or *kiruv* group, they are available. Based in Israel, you can contact them at Sarah.tikvah1@gmail.com or at 052-528-1207.

174. She is available through her website joybreaksbarriers.com.

175. As featured in *Ami Magazine*, Feb. 20, 2013.

176. As reported in *Ami-Living*, Adar 5773, p. 108.

177. Sara Chana resides in New Jersey, but travels to bring Comedy Cures' life-affirming work to ill patients and families throughout the US and world. Saranne has helped almost 700,000 people at more than 700 live events rediscover their funny bones through her motivational, inspirational, laughter-rich performances and unique therapeutic productions. See ComedyCures.org.

178. *Mesilas Yesharim*, Shaar HaTaharah, end: *Achar ha'peulos nimshachim ha'levovos*.

179. Also attributed to Norman Vincent Peale.

180. http://www.ted.com/talks/amy_cuddy_your_body_language_shapes_who_you_are.

181. *Ha'adam nifal kefi pe'ulosav* — A person is drawn towards his external activities. *Sefer HaChinuch, parshas Bo*, mitzva 16. See also our section on Power Poses.

182. Available at www.zipidagan.co.il.

183. Dr. Lee Berk and Dr. Stanley Tan of Loma Linda University in California have achieved prominence for their studies on the effects of laughter on the immune system. They, and others, have found many positive benefits for laughter (generated either through humor or mechanical laughter).

184. Bernie Siegel, MD, internationally recognized expert in the field of cancer treatment and complementary, holistic medicine, writes on the relationship between the patient and the healing process.

185. Known to some as the father of author Sarah Shapiro.

186. Originally published 1979 by W. W. Norton & Co.

187. P. 155.

188. http://medical-dictionary.thefreedictionary.com/Stress.

189. Susan Dubinsky.

190. Arnold Glasow.

191. John Morreall, www.humorworks.com.

192. John Morreal, video, humorworks.com. A mirthful humor-laughter experience is a eustress positive phenomenon and ameliorates biological effects of distress. Four negative biological reactions are reversed with humor. The body-systems that are depressed through distress are enhanced through humor. http://www.fasebj.org/cgi/content/meeting_abstract/22/1_MeetingAbstracts/946.11.

193. Peter Ustinov.

194. Carr & Greeves, *Only Joking* (Gotham Books, 2006), p. 272.

195. *Makkos* 24b.

196. Program director of Counterforce and clinical director of a Telephone Help Line.

197. Ibid.

198. Viktor Frankl's method is called logotherapy. *Logos* means "meaning" in Greek. He believed that man can detach from situations, himself, choose an attitude about himself, and determine his own determinants, thus shaping his own character and becoming responsible for himself.

199. Gordon Allport, *The Individual and His Religion*.

200. http://en.wikipedia.org/wiki/Logotherapy.

201. Quoted by Rav Elazar Koenig, as seen in "Finding Happiness in Breslov," *Ami Magazine*, Adar II, 5774.

202. The lower brain governs basic life through the primitive reflexes that dominate at birth, and also controls motor and sensory functions.

203. http://www.britannica.com/EBchecked/topic/276309/humour.

204. http://www.medlink.com/medlinkcontent.asp. Communication deficits associated with right-hemisphere injury involve non-literal language (e.g., metaphor, irony, and indirect requests), humor and story comprehension, and the ability to inference.

205. www.humorworks.com. Dr. Morreall is an internationally recognized authority on humor and its benefits. See his *15 Ways to Accomplish More With the Right Kind of Humor* (Kare Anderson), available at Forbes.com.

206. Rebbetzin Chaya Mushka Schneerson.

207. Derived from a Greek word which means "beyond expectation."

208. An author known for his surprise endings.

209. http://www.britannica.com/EBchecked/topic/276309/humour/11919/The-logic-of-laughter#toc11920.

210. Encyclopedia Britannica, ibid.

211. Bill Nye.

212. The room measured ten cubits long, and the Holy Ark was two-and-a-half cubits long. Inexplicably, the distance from each wall to the Holy Ark was measured five cubits.

213. Translated from Yiddish. Unfortunately I can't give credit to its author. It circulated via WhatsApp.

214. http://www.quotegarden.com/technology.html.

215. Definitions from Google.com.

216. Brian Seaward, *Managing Stress*, 7th edition (Jones & Bartlett Publishers, 2011), p. 177.

217. http://www.britannica.com/EBchecked/topic/276309/humour/11924/Situational-humour.

218. Carr & Greeves. p. 200. Note that this evaluation is offered in / made by a non-Jewish "objective" source.

219. Romain Gary.

220. Seen in "What's So Funny," *Mishpacha* magazine, Adar II, 5765. [The author's name could not be traced].

221. Arland Ussher.

222. Carr & Greeves, p. 21.

223. Max Eastman.

224. Taken from an article by Lord Dr. Jonathan Sachs, as seen in *Algemeiner Journal*, March 18, 2011.

225. p. 43.

226. p. 41.

227. Kurt Vonnegut.

228. Puzant Kevork Thomajan.

229. See our chapter on "Origins of Laughter."

230. "What you get when you laugh," from *The Healing Power of Humor* by Allen Klein.

231. Alfred Stern, "Why do we laugh and cry?"

232. Yeshayah 25:8.

233. Adapted from *The Scroll*, a weekly publication by chabad.org.

234. A child who speaks and acts normally at home but is tight-lipped in the school setting.

235. From a video clip that my daughter captured.

236. http://theyeshiva.net/Article/View/111/The-Greatest-Joke.

237. In the videotape, exclamations of surprise and delight are heard as the bystanders' brains unscramble the link between the mysterious disappearance of the man and the sudden appearance of the two dancers.

238. Bereishis 21:6.

239. Equivalent numerical totals — *gematrios* — signify a relationship between ideas.

240. *Overcoming Folly*, translated by Rabbi Zalman Posner (Kehot Publication Society).

241. We're not speaking of witty humor, but rather the idea of incongruity, the novelty that activates our funny bone.

242. Sacrifices are reported in Torah as providing for G-d a *rei'ach nichoach*, a pleasing fragrance, and *nachas ruach*, pleasurable.

243. *Torah Or, parshas Vayishlach*, p. 50.

244. Tehillim 2:4. See "Redeeming Laughter" by Akiva Tatz on chabad.org.

245. *Sotah* 3a.

246. *Iggeres Hakodesh, Lessons in Tanya* 4, p. 322.

247. *Kesubos* 17a.

248. He would dance holding myrtle branches.

249. Elbert Hubbard.

250. The readiness to sacrifice does not refer only to the giving up of one's life. It includes a readiness to sacrifice and to undergo hardships to follow the laws described in the Torah, or dedicate our lives to a greater good. For example: Ada was "going kosher." She had to give up her beautiful china, her favorite restaurant dishes, and much of her social life was impacted, since its nature is to revolve heavily around food.

251. Shoshana Troppe.

252. Rabbi Shlomo Goldman, Rebbe of Zivhil.

253. From a lecture by Rabbi Shlomo Majeski, "*shtus d'kedusha*," subject archive 22 Shevat, nsheichabadcentral.org.

254. Tehillim 126:2.

255. Bereishis 19:4.

256. ArtScroll Bereishis, p. 182.

257. Bereishis 17:17.

258. Ibid. 18:12.

259. Gutnick Chumash, p. 105.

260. Bereishis 21:6.

261. Rashi ad loc.

262. "...and you will name him Yitzchak." Bereishis 17:19.

263. Ibid. 21:12.

264. *Zohar* 1:122b. Discussed elaborately on audio recordings by Rabbi Yossi Paltiel, at inside-chassidus.org, *parshas Chayei Sarah*. Also at http://www.kabbalaonline.org/kabbalah/article_cdo/aid/379339/jewish/The-Complete-Joy-of-Sarah.htm. There are several variations of this theme. See also sefer *Maamorim Melukat* II, p. 145-152.

265. As we say in Kiddush on Friday night: *asher bara...la'asos*. That word means to perfect, like *l'takein*. G-d created a world and then created Man. We are partners in his endeavor to complete this world together.

266. Literally, royalty or kingship; the last of the ten creative attributes of G-d called *sefiros*. G-d reveals Himself through those *sefiros*.

267. As seen in "Happiness in Breslov," *Ami* magazine, March 12, 2014.

268. Achor, *Happiness Advantage*, p. 52.

269. Elizabeth Dunn, http://www.nytimes.com/2014/05/11/travel/what-a-great-trip-and-im-not-even-there-yet.html?

270. *A Treasury of Chassidic Tales on the Torah*, by Rabbi Zevin.

271. *Re'u* means "see" [my pain]; *shima* because G-d "heard," her misery; *levi* means to bond or accompany, expressing her longing for stronger connection with her husband.

272. From the word *hoda'a*, which means gratitude.

273. Note: a *shammes* is a respectable position, but it often barely pays the rent.

274. Presentation at Nefesh Conference, Dec 2007.

275. Isaiah HaLevi Horovitz (c. 1565 – March 24, 1630), also known as the Shelah HaKadosh (the holy Shelah) after the title of his best-known work, was a prominent Levite rabbi and mystic.

276. Shemos 15:1.

277. Rashi ad loc.

278. Shelah, parshas Beshalach.

279. *Taanis* 29a.

280. Elul 11, 5752.

281. Equivalent numerical totals (*gematrios*) signify a link between words and concepts. This number-linking has significance when it is presented by a leading Torah authority and a meticulous adherent of its practices. The word *az* consists of two letters — *aleph* has the numerical value one and *zayin* equals seven.

282. We begin counting generations from the Baal Shem Tov, who established joy as the cornerstone to serving G-d.

283. The Baal Shem Tov passed away in 1760. A generation is usually twenty years.

284. As reported by Tzipi Dagan.

285. Nicholas Sparks.

286. Facts compiled by Ball Memorial Hospital in Muncie, Indiana.

287. Berk, Tan, Fry, et al. "Neuroendocrine and stress hormone changes during mirthful laughter." *American Journal of Medical Science* (1989, 298): 390–396.

288. Paul E. McGhee, Ph.D., The Laughter Remedy.

Dedicated to the release of Sholom Mordechai haLevi Rubashkin.
We join with him in blissful anticipation, with joyous certainty
and *bitachon*, that he will be dancing together with his brethren
around the world with the joy of his personal *geulah* and the
geulah of *acheinu Bnei Yisrael* very, very soon.

About the Author

Gitty Stolik writes on Jewish thought and lore for a variety of Jewish publications. Her articles are popular for exploring content-rich topics of timeless value in an engaging style. She is also the editor of *Our Vogue*, a publication with insights on the values of modesty for women and girls (archives can be viewed at ourvogue.org). Her writings are used as informational resources around the world. This is her first book.

When she's not writing about joy and other topics, Mrs. Stolik applies the magic of joy and positivity to the field of education, in particular to the learning- and language-disabled population. She is striving to add an M.S. (Mastery of Simchah) to her academic titles.

The author also speaks on a variety of inspirational topics. She has been humorously dubbed the "Lemonade Therapist" for her special dose of perspective flip-overs.

About Mosaica Press

Mosaica Press is an independent publisher of Jewish books. Our authors include some of the most profound, interesting, and entertaining thinkers and writers in the Jewish community today. There is a great demand for high-quality Jewish works dealing with issues of the day — and Mosaica Press is helping fill that need. Our books are available around the world. Please visit us at www.mosaicapress.com or contact us at info@mosaicapress.com. We will be glad to hear from you.

MOSAICA PRESS